MW01490024

THE
AWARE
LEADER

Self-Knowledge is the KEY to Your Success

RICHARD METHENY

THE AWARE LEADER

DALLAS, TEXAS

Copyright © 2020 by Richard Metheny

All rights reserved. No part of this publication may be reproduced, distributed, or transmitted in any form or by any means, including photocopying, recording, or other electronic or mechanical methods, without the prior written permission of the publisher, except in the case of brief quotations embodied in critical reviews and certain other noncommercial uses permitted by copyright law. For permission requests, write to the publisher at the address below.

ISBN (paperback): 978-1-65311-821-2

The Aware Leader LLC
638 Turner Avenue
Dallas, Texas 75208
richard@theawareleader.com
www.theawareleader.com

Cover design by Graham Publishing Group
Text design and composition by John Reinhardt Book Design

Printed in the United States of America

A Note to Readers

Although the case studies in this book are drawn from my actual coaching experiences, some names and situations have been modified to protect client identities and to make their stories clearer for readers to follow.

To Mom, who is still my best life coach,

and to Aunt Mildred,

who instilled in me a zeal for books.

CONTENTS

INTRODUCTION

It Really Is Who You Know

What have you done so far in your life to set the stage for lasting success? Throughout your youth, you prepared for a career by attending school and filling yourself with *knowledge*. Early job searches taught you that you also needed to gather *experience*. As you've built your career, you and your employers have invested in the development of your *skills*. Amid all that, you've discovered that networking with mentors, colleagues, and people in power has been crucial to developing your cache as a leader. Despite all that, if you're like most leaders, you're not aware of the one person with the inside information that can make or break you in Corporate America, information no one else will ever tell you. If you don't get to know that person, you will probably fail to fulfill your aspirations.

> *To be an effective leader, you must wake to a new awareness: that the person you most need to know is you.*

1

When I met Gail, she had worked her way up the corporate ladder to the C-suite of a global technology company. Gail had worked hard to develop her knowledge, experience, and skills. She had developed important relationships, but she had spent almost no time developing a relationship with herself. Her lack of self-awareness was a disaster waiting to happen.

Experience has taught me that the lack of a clear sense of self almost always has its roots in childhood. I don't need to be a psychologist to recognize the way someone's personal story can impact their career, I only need to take an interest in learning that story. As a child, Gail had grown up believing that the only way she could elicit loving responses from her father was by succeeding at everything she did. When she won academic contests in elementary school, when she won at high school sports, when she received her acceptance letter from a premier university, her father showered her with affection. When she failed, he ignored her.

As an adult, Gail continued to be "Daddy's good little girl" by successfully running many projects and businesses, acquiring material wealth, and projecting an image of achievement. The problem was, she did not understand what drove her: the ongoing need to gain her father's approval. Without knowing why, she lived by an inner rule that told her to achieve every goal at any cost. She had to win or she would feel worthless. Losing was not an option.

"Many organizations are run like that," you might say. "What's wrong with it?" On the face of it, not much. Except that Gail's burning drive for success led her to multiple divorces and to signing one multi-million-dollar venture after another, until she was finally presented with the deal to end all deals. She saw herself and her company as dominating their competitive sphere, which led her to overestimate the value of the deal and underestimate the role of chance and circumstance in its success. Her internal drive to succeed at all costs also blinded her to many warning signs that the deal was not solid. Most glaring was that the business she was acquiring was in an oversaturated market.

Even though she had good intentions, Gail broke her company, along with many business relationships along the way. You might think, "I have more sense than that. It would never happen to me." Gail, too, was certain that her business sense was solid. She did not know what she did not know. Gail was unaware of her internal drivers, so she had no strategy to deal with them.

When you don't know who you are, you take away your power to choose what to do.

We all grow up learning to cope with less than perfect formative environments provided by family, teachers, friends, and significant others. Our coping mechanisms, some good, some not so good, help us survive. But when we move beyond survival to leadership, we cannot afford to let unconscious motivations push us around the way they did when we were kids.

We all reach a point in life when we make decisions and take actions without being aware of why. People who do not engage in self-awareness just keep on doing this. With the exception of sheer luck, those people are cruising straight toward failure at the first unexpected bump in the road. It's only a matter of time.

Build Yourself a Better Path to Leadership

Corporate America spends most of its leadership development money on finding and growing talent with the best experience, skills, and knowledge for their field. That endeavor is a sixty-billion-dollar industry. But *experience, skills,* and *knowledge* only comprise half the tools in your leadership toolkit. The other half is made up of *behavior, styles, and preferences.* Those last three tools provide the fuel that drives the way you use the first three. Yet corporations invest very little to help leaders develop an awareness of those three personal drivers. That, even though research repeatedly shows that more than half of all executives fail, usually because of one of those three things: behavior, styles, and preferences.

Think about the executive failures you hear about in the news. They rarely happen because those corporate executives did not have experience, skills, or knowledge. It's almost always because of their behavior.

*In my more than 4000 hours coaching executives, one common denominator has become abundantly clear to me: self-awareness in leaders is not merely a helpful asset. It is **the deciding factor** in their success.*

Unlike knowledge, experience, and skills, you don't need any special education or training to gain behavior, styles, and preferences. You already have them, whether you want them or not. However, if you don't know what they are or how to use them, you're in trouble. You're like a soldier carrying explosives, unaware they're rattling around in your toolkit with the power to blow up your career at any time. The thing is, if only you knew what to do with them, you could also be responsible for the most exciting fireworks show your company has ever seen. The difference between becoming that unwitting bomber versus that cool pyrotechnician lies in one thing: getting to know yourself.

The failure of most of Corporate America to invest in developing self-awareness in its leadership is losing companies big money, costing leaders important opportunities, and contributing to a culture of misery for the workforce at large. I believe this signals a huge untapped opportunity, both for companies and the individuals who lead them.

In 2013, research analysts David Zes and Dana Landis of Korn Ferry Institute conducted a study that provides hard data linking business success to higher self-awareness in individuals.[1]1 The researchers analyzed 6,977 self-assessments from professionals at 486 publicly traded companies to identify "blind spots"—that is, disparities between the individuals' self-reported skills and the ratings their peers gave them on those same skills. The frequency of blind spots was measured against the stock performance of those companies. Their research found the following:

- Poorly performing companies' employees had 20% more blind spots than those working at financially strong companies.
- Poorly performing companies' employees were 79% more likely to have low overall self-awareness than those at firms with a robust rate of return.

From "A Better Return on Self-Awareness," by David Zes, Ph.D. and Dana Landis, Ph.D., Korn Ferry Institute

For most people, there is a disparity between the way they see themselves and the way others see them. This causes many leaders to overestimate their strengths, ignore feedback, and deny their shortcomings. In some cases, it causes leaders to do the opposite: underestimate their strengths, internalize the criticism of others, and overemphasize their shortcomings. Either way, the results are the same: unaware leaders inevitably damage their own reputations.

The key to success is bringing your personal identity in line with your reputation. This requires the self-examination that leads to self-awareness.

Okay, so if you want to increase self-awareness, how do you do it? You might think your best bet is to look to game-changers in modern business for answers, such as the CEOs on Fortune's annual list of the World's 50 Greatest Leaders.

CEOs on Fortune's list of The World's 50 Greatest Leaders, 2018

- Tim Cook
- Marc Bebioff
- Oprah Winfrey
- Jamie Dimon
- Daniel Servitje Montull
- Feike Sijbesma
- Mukesh Ambani
- Ana Botin
- Huateng "Pony" Ma

- Mary Barra
- Larry Fink
- Kenneth Frazier

Might they be able to help you on this subject? *Nope.* No doubt the above list is full of great leaders to learn from, but none of them can bring you one step closer to knowing *yourself.* This is not about some one-size-fits-all technique or ideology. This is about you. You're the one who needs to ask the questions, and you're the only one who can come up with the answers.

What Randy Didn't Know

The importance of knowing yourself is not new. In fact, it's ancient. The Ancient Greek aphorism "Know thyself" is one of the Delphic maxims inscribed in the forecourt of the Temple of Apollo at Delphi. In 1734, Alexander Pope wrote the poem "An Essay on Man, Epistle II," which begins: "Know then thyself, presume not God to scan; The proper study of mankind is Man." In 1902, Hugo von Hofmannsthal wrote *The Letter of Lord Chandos*, a fictional letter from his sixteenth-century alter ego, Lord Chandos, to Francis Bacon, in which he mentions an intention to write a book called *"Nosce te ipsum,"* which is Latin for "Know thyself." In the 1999 movie, *The Matrix,* Lana and Andy Wachowski posted another variation of that maxim, *temet nosce,* on a plaque over the door of the Oracle.

References to the time-honored quest to "know thyself" are legion. Being open to and applying that knowledge is another story.

Randy had a proven record of leadership in the insurance industry, yet he still got himself in hot water when he reached the top. Why?

The board of directors at his company sure didn't see it coming. They had hired Randy because he had always shown a solid commitment to both members and employees. He had all the things most boards look for in a CEO: a pedigree education, broad experience, and the skills of an industry thought-leader. What's more, Randy was charismatic and great with the media. He took his post during a time of regulatory reform, which gave him a platform to show off his public relations skills by entering a public debate. He soon became a sought-after media darling.

What the board did not know was that Randy was on a mission to leave a legacy, to make his personal mark on the industry by shaping the new world order for insurance companies. This was not a mission in service to the company's goals, but to his own ego. Randy probably did not see his motives that way, because the evidence indicates Randy did not know his true self.

Over four years, Randy became less involved in operating the company and more involved in developing and implementing plans to ensure his legacy. At first, it appeared he was simply an independent leader, but his approach soon evolved into ostracizing, even bullying, his executive team and withholding information from the board. Cracks in Randy's charisma began to show, revealing emotional volatility, narcissism, defensiveness, and excessive self-reliance.

Randy's options grew narrower until his company began to show the symptoms of its leader's problem. Although the company grew in revenue and membership, the increases did not translate into net income gains. In fact, the company began to see significant losses. One of his riskiest strategies included unethical contractual agreements with vendors.

Everything came to a head when Randy's risky endeavor resulted in an eighty-million-dollar loss in 2014. For a person interested in self-knowledge, this would have been a wake-up call to stop and take stock of who he was, why he was doing what he was doing, and what steps he could take to realign his external actions with his internal values. But Randy was not a look-inward kind of guy. When he saw his legacy in jeopardy, instead of reevaluating the direction of his life, he looked for accounting maneuvers to hide the company's losses. Instead of looking at himself, he blamed others. Randy's self-deception was profound.

By the time Randy called me to consult with him, it was too late. He insisted we meet in a different city. I later learned this was so nobody from his company would find out he was seeking outside help. He did not tell me the whole story, but he did say he was seeking ways to cover his mistakes by using creative accounting on the balance sheet. It was clear he was on ethically shaky ground. "That sounds risky," I said. "What do you think about that?" But he didn't want to think about it, he just wanted to make all his problems go away with as little inconvenience to himself as possible. He was the epitome of the unaware leader.

Several months later the board fired him for cause, without severance. In one day, he went from making more than half-a-million dollars a year to zero. Randy again became a media favorite, but for all the wrong reasons.

What John Knew

Then I met John, who did not look nearly as good on paper as Randy did. Today John is a successful Chief Financial Officer for a medium-sized logistics company in the South. People describe him as "refreshing. A CFO whose first reply is not to say, 'No.'" Unlike Randy, John was not an obvious choice for his position. Oh, his experience, skills, and knowledge made him look like a good match at first glance, but I did an assessment of John's leadership competencies and he scored "low potential" on a key *six* out of sixteen. We spent two hours discussing his assessment, and I was impressed by one important thing: it did not upset him. In fact, he was not surprised to hear that one competency in which he scored low involved his ability to earn loyalty and trust.

"I know that," John said. "I've known it for a long time."

John told me a story about his days as a youth minister. His mentor, a church pastor, had a talk with John one day and explained that while his desire for achievement was admirable, he was overplaying it. The pastor gave him the hard truth: that his abrupt, insensitive style was likely to kill his future. "If you keep treating people the way you do, keep chasing what you want without stopping to think about what other people need, I'm afraid you won't have the success in life that you want."

That was an awakening for John. "I realized that deep down inside I was trying so hard to please my hard-to-please father that it overshadowed my focus on other people."

That epiphany did not change John on the inside. He was still ambitious and still found it difficult to be sensitive to others. That's a permanent part of his makeup. But knowing about that part of himself gave him the choice to learn strategies to deal with it.

John developed a vision of who he wanted to be and how he wanted to actualize that vision of himself. He focused on observing himself and becoming aware of triggers that might set off his insensitivity. He learned to recognize when his drive for achievement supported his vision and when it didn't. What's more, he had strong values and he used those values to filter his decisions. John accepted that he could not eliminate his urge to achieve at all costs, but he could be more aware of when those urges were likely to show their ugly side.

The key difference between John and Randy is not that John was predisposed to be a better leader, but that he was aware of who he was and why. Randy did not know himself, so he did not have the power to make informed choices about his behavior. Randy made blind choices, unaware of why he did what he did or what the impact might be. By contrast, John was an aware leader. Does John still make bad choices sometimes? Yes. Are they minimalized? Of course.

How accurate is your self-image? Are you aware of how you came to be who you are? Are you aware of what you value and how it shapes your thoughts? Are you aware of how your thoughts lead to action? Are you aware of the way others see you? How do you show up in the world as a spouse, parent, friend, son, daughter, leader, peer, or member of your community? Asking such questions is an excellent first step on the path to getting to know yourself.

Awareness is the path of immortality;
thoughtlessness is the path of death.
Those who are aware do not die.
The thoughtless are as if dead already.

The wise having clearly understood this, delight in awareness
and find joy in the knowledge of the noble ones.
These wise ones, meditative, persevering, always using strong effort,
attain nirvana, the supreme peace and happiness.

—BUDDHA

Self-Awareness Is Not About Strengths and Weaknesses

The field of leadership development is filled with expert information describing the behaviors, competencies, or attributes it takes to be a good leader. One of the most popular perennial leadership topics is "knowing your strengths and weaknesses." In this book, I will *not* adopt that kind of dichotomy, because I believe it's counterproductive to think of leadership traits in terms of "good or bad," "strengths or weaknesses," "positive or negative." People often set up these black-and-white comparisons to make things easier to grasp, to create simple stories about ourselves that we can easily understand. Fifteen years of coaching leaders has proven to me that self-awareness is more complicated than that.

Productive self-awareness does not require figuring out what's wrong with you or right with you, does not require positive versus negative thinking, does not divide you into "keep" and "discard" piles. Self-awareness challenges you to engage in neutral thinking, to look at your attributes, thoughts, and behaviors—without judgment. (I'm not talking about the kind of judgment we use when it comes to taking actions in which we might knowingly harm ourselves or others, which is a necessary form of judgment.) Consider the opportunities that might open to you, if you could recognize how various aspects of your makeup sometimes facilitate success and at other times hinder success. Consider how empowering it might be if you understood how every one of your qualities can be either a benefit or a hindrance, depending on the situation.

Many of us mistake self-criticism for self-awareness. It's all too easy to attempt a journey of self-reflection, only to fall into the crippling trap of self-judgment. A lack of compassion for self can lead to self-condemnation, which is not at all empowering for leaders. By the same token, constant self-affirmation is not true self-awareness either. That can lead to self-aggrandizement, which can cause a false sense of confidence.

Self-awareness requires neutral thinking.
As long as you see self-discovery as judging
yourself in terms of "good" versus "bad," you
are not getting to know the real you.

Neutral thinking is the key: Who have I been, who am I now, who do I want to be? What do I bring to the table, when does it work, when doesn't it work? Who am I on the inside, who am I on the outside, and how can I make them match?

Neutral thinking is not indifference or lack of conviction. It is at its best unbiased and objective. It leads you to listen to all sides of a question and consider what others think. Neutral thinking involves detachment from emotions, but it does not mean you need to become uncaring. Instead, it means keeping your emotions in check so they don't take you by surprise and lead to knee-jerk reactions. Neutral thinking allows you to ask questions, seek information, and consider alternatives, without rushing to judgment. In neutral thinking, you respond authentically and effectively to events rather than wasting energy trying to bend events to your will. In neutral thinking, you consider the potential long-term effects of your choices.

The more you engage in neutral thinking, the more you are *at choice* about your behavior, improving the opportunity to be an effective leader. When you are *at choice*, you can clearly see every path before you. When you can identify the past stories that influence you, the mental processes that guide you, and the behaviors that you repeat, you will discover a new power. Not the power to *change* who you are, but rather the power to *make more informed and effective choices* within the context of who you are.

A Ship With a Rudder

I've worked with executives who dismiss the need to develop the psychological aspects of leadership. Such executives typically have low self-awareness. I wonder if that's ego at work: if they avoid looking within, then they don't have to face uncomfortable information about themselves. Some may dread finding out they're not as perfect as they hoped, or worse, that they're just as flawed as they feared. If we engage in neutral thinking, we neutralize this issue. It's not about what's right or wrong with us, but about learning what we have in hand so we can leverage it.

I find it curious that some leaders scoff at internal awareness as a touchy-feely, hippy-dippy exercise in "getting in touch with your inner child instead of just bucking up and doing what needs to be done." To such leaders, I suggest that trying to tough-out life in the big office without knowing what's going on inside you is like trying to sail a ship without knowing where the rudder is and how to operate it.

On the other hand, it strikes me as normal to be disinclined to spend much time on self-reflection. After all, it's not easy. As Lily Tomlin once said, "Self-knowledge isn't necessarily good news." Even when *someone else* gives us feedback, it's difficult to be open to it because it's not always flattering. But this book is aimed at leaders, and leaders cannot afford to shy away from doing the hard thing if the hard thing will get results. Time and again, I've seen self-awareness lead to results. As we become more self-aware, we become better at identifying opportunities for professional development and personal growth.

SELF-AWARENESS YIELDS BENEFITS THAT WILL MAKE YOU AN EVEN MORE EFFECTIVE LEADER:

- Accepting that you don't know everything, that you can't do everything, and that hiding weaknesses only highlights them—which frees you to be authentic and stop pretending
- Giving permission to others to collaborate without fear of appearing unqualified
- Gaining more trust from others, which increases your credibility

- Soliciting feedback that allows you to see yourself as others do, which gives you more information on the skills and relationships in your toolkit
- Walking an inspirational path of continuous learning
- Growing more flexible and confident in your approach to leadership
- Dealing with challenges in a more positive, less anxious way
- Communicating more effectively
- Reducing stress
- Improving your decision process

SELF-AWARENESS YIELDS BENEFITS THAT WILL HELP YOU LIVE A MORE FULFILLING LIFE:

- Choosing conscious actions instead of merely reacting
- Genuinely loving yourself
- Enjoying authentic fulfillment rather than pretending to be happy
- Gaining greater depth of experience
- Redirecting negative thoughts and emphasizing positive ones
- Choosing behaviors that increase your options instead of derailing your goals
- Building positive interpersonal relationships
- Being the real you
- Living courageously
- Transforming your dreams from fantasy to reality

Wherever you are in your career, now is a perfect time to start your journey to becoming an aware leader. I was forty-five when I began to get to know myself—a story I'll tell you later—and I'm still a beginner. I'm sixty now. If you do the math, that tells you I spent two-thirds of my life semiconscious. What I used to call "being aware" was just me listening to my internal critic. That critic constantly told me I must avoid letting anybody find out I was a screw-up, by doing everything I could to prevent failure. Preventing failure looked like success to the world, but it never felt like success to me. My career and my life did not take off, internally or externally, until I became self-aware, gave up pretending, and risked putting my true self out there.

Self-awareness starts with knowing you are unique. Only you can be who you are. So the more you know about you, the greater your opportunity to make contributions nobody else can make. My goal in writing this book is to give you tools and ideas to support you in doing what I cannot do for you: exploring yourself. I hope when you're done reading it you'll be on the road to a more conscious, self-empowered mind.

I propose a challenge to you: by the end of this book, be prepared to name one thing you plan to do to put your self-awareness into action and become an even more effective leader.

As a fellow traveler on the journey to become an aware leader, I can tell you: knowing yourself is not for the complacent. This will take hard work, but I promise it is rewarding work that will pay you back many times over. If you want to be a more powerful leader in the front office and in life, then self-awareness is the key. So join me, and let's open the door.

ONE

THE BUSINESS OF SELF-AWARENESS

The Journey of a Lifetime

I finally made it to the executive ranks, promoted to vice president at a twenty-billion-dollar company. It took me until my forties, but hey, I was there. Still, I was not happy at the top. That same year I went through a divorce. It seemed I could never get the sun, moon, and stars to align in my favor.

Something had to change.

My transition to V.P. required me to go through executive coaching. I made a commitment to myself to take full advantage of this opportunity, to learn about myself and how to become more effective in all areas of my life. As part of that commitment, I also chose to undergo therapy. It was one of the hardest things I've ever done, but one of the most positive life-changing decisions I've ever made. In fact, Dr. Irving Gadol guided me to a pivotal realization that led me to become the kind of leader I never knew I always wanted to be.

Dr. Gadol asked the question that would change everything for me: "Would you describe yourself?"

One of the first words I used was "introspective."

He said, "No, you're not."

"Excuse me?"

"You're not introspective. You're highly self-critical."

At first I politely denied it. But after our session, I thought, "Okay, let's accept that his statement is correct. What does that mean?" Actually, it explained a lot. It gave me a context to think about why I was not sleeping well, why I ruminated endlessly about problems long past, why I criticized myself daily for not doing things perfectly, and why I had a couple of angry outbursts a year in the wrong place at the wrong time. All of which probably had prevented me from becoming a V.P. in my thirties. That was the beginning of a personal exploration that is not over to this day.

My inner self-critic did not vanish. That guy has lived in my head since I was a kid and he's not moving out. But I did learn to effectively deal with him, by becoming an aware leader.

Starting my journey to self-awareness effected change in all aspects of my leadership, launching me into a successful career in the C-suite. I was so inspired by the tangible results that I wanted to share what I had learned with other leaders, not as a therapist but in a capacity that would call on my own leadership skills. I became an executive human resource leader, committed to spreading the word that self-awareness and success are inseparable. By 2006, I had worked with so many leaders who discovered success through self-awareness that it inspired me to enter the Georgetown University Leadership Coaching certification program and become a certified leadership coach.

I now coach clients at the executive level and in the C-suite, supporting them through their personal journeys as they discover how self-awareness can improve their effectiveness and, therefore, the bottom line of their companies. Most of my clients tell me that discovering new ways of seeing themselves has opened them to opportunities they never before knew. They're discovering that what I propose to them is true: if you want to succeed at the top, then the person you need to know most is *you*.

You Model Your Company's Success

We all have a way of looking at ourselves. But I have discovered most leaders don't look at the way they look at themselves. Sometimes they do invest in awareness opportunities for other people who work for them, but corporate culture must be modeled. According to research from multinational management consultants McKinsey & Company, about half of all efforts to transform organizations fail, either because senior managers don't act like role models for change or because organization members resist change.[3]

As McKinsey puts it: "Organizations don't change. People change."

If an organization wants to stay on the path of success, that is to say, on the path of change and growth, then the people who make up that organization are the ones who must change and grow. It takes leaders to lead change, and the leaders who are best at it are the ones who know the most about who they are and what makes them tick. The leaders I coach have proven again and again what Kinsey has also discovered: external company strategies for change are hit-and-miss, unless they are linked to company leaders engaging in efforts of internal self-discovery.

Experience has taught me that the most important interaction in any organization is always between two people. That's it: just two. That's where ideas begin to roll in the direction you want them to go, or begin to roll the opposite way. What makes that kind of interaction either succeed or break down comes down to this: every time you throw two people together, they each have different needs, objectives, and beliefs. One factor makes those interactions as productive as they can be: each person having intimate knowledge, not of each other, but of themselves. Even if only one of the pair is operating at that level, they have a better shot than most leaders, because most leaders have not yet glommed onto the proven results of the ancient quest for self.

Why does the examined life make the difference? It's a pretty straightforward trajectory: the more we know ourselves, the more we know how we impact others; the more we know how we impact others, the more choices we have about how to leverage that impact; and the more we can leverage that impact, the more we can influence others in a way that promotes positive change. Positive change leads to results, which leads to growth.

If you go into any venture, project, or partnership without knowing yourself, then your choices will be limited and your results will be random. It might all turn out great, or it might not. Wouldn't you like to improve those odds?

A Keystone in Your Organization's Success

As an executive, you're intent on changing your marketplace. Business performance is important to you. You would not be where you are if you were not diligent about focusing yourself and your team on the innovations that lead to success. New discoveries in neuroscience show that the self-aware brain is a powerful engine for change in the business world.

Maybe you have already set the wheels in motion to ensure that your top people develop into aware leaders. However, if you are anything like most top leaders when I first encounter them, you likely spend little time working to understand and change *yourself*. If so, you're missing a keystone in building a bridge to company-wide change. If you don't do your own internal work, it's possible for everything else to fall apart.

It might seem tough to find time to think about who you are, about your drivers, habits, and values. Perhaps you, like many executives, are not inclined to self-reflect. Maybe you believe you can't change, or don't want to change because the person you are has gotten this far. Maybe you're uncomfortable with, or lack confidence in, feedback from others, especially if they work below you and might have an axe to grind or see you as a posterior they need to kiss.

Why should you invest in getting to know yourself? After all, you're not running an encounter group; you're running a business. Is there a business case for self-awareness?

I assure you, there is. Research conducted in 2010 by Green Peak Partners and Cornell's School of Industrial and Labor Relations looked at 72 executives, and they concluded that high self-awareness correlates with achieving high degrees of success as a leader. Per the research: "Interestingly, a high self-awareness score was the strongest predictor of overall success. This is not altogether surprising as executives who are aware of their weaknesses are often better able to hire subordinates who perform well in categories in which the leader lacks acumen. These leaders are also more able to entertain the idea that someone on their team may have an idea that is even better than their own."

"Leadership searches give short shrift to 'self-awareness,' which should actually be a top criterion." — Green Peak Partners and Cornell's School of Industrial and Labor Relations[4]

I often encounter clients at the point when their lack of self-awareness has begun to affect their performance. One former client, whom I'll call Denise, had been chosen by a global advertising agency to manage a big change. By Green Peak Partners' research standard, that would call for her to have a high level of self-awareness. Instead, Denise's self-awareness was so low she wasn't even aware of what she was unaware of. As the leader of a new office in Southeast Asia, she was sure she knew what the job required: she quickly identified key priorities and mobilized the needed resources to execute sales results. However, Denise did not know an important thing about herself: her admirable drive and focus often led her to overextend her team. Denise was unaware that her leadership style was hindering her team members from change and growth.

What didn't Denise know?

On many occasions she would hand out projects she believed needed to be done, without pausing to consider the individual skill levels, readiness, or conflicting priorities of the people she assigned. She often knew the result she wanted, but failed to clearly articulate the specifics of what it would take to get there. She failed to empower her team members to achieve anything beyond what she required, yet still somehow managed to burn them out.

There was a serious disconnect between the way Denise saw herself and the way her employees saw her. While she saw herself as a leader who involved her staff in resolving daily issues, employees described her style as "drive-by shootings." Her team grew frustrated with her lack of communication, while Denise grew frustrated with their lack of performance. A more self-aware leader would have seen her own frustration as a signal to stop and assess what was going on with her and with them. Instead, she shoved down her irritation and took over more tasks to make up for what she believed her team "lacked." This only made things worse.

Because Denise only looked outward and not inward for causes, she was unaware of her role in the problem. When she looked at herself, she focused on the fact that she was successful with clients, who loved her energy, creativity, and "get it done" approach. But *selling* work was not the issue, *executing* work was.

Denise's office soon ranked the lowest in employee engagement and the highest in employee turnover among twelve global offices. She chalked up the high employee churn to a cultural rite of passage for "walkabouts," that is to say "young employees on the lookout for new experiences in work and travel."

I met Denise when her agency invited my company to put regional office leaders through a leadership assessment that included 360-feedback—that is, feedback from those who worked around each leader. Denise was happy, and not surprised, to know that her employees loved her drive and her ability to bring in business. She was, however, dismayed to learn that her focus on advancement led her to come across with a blunt, insensitive interpersonal style and a low awareness of employee needs. Most of the time her team members had no idea what she thought of their performance until things went wrong and she "let them have it."

As difficult as it was for Denise to hear that feedback, she took it to heart. She began to take a proactive approach in facilitating her staff's professional development. She considered people's readiness for assignments and set clear expectations so they could better track their progress. She stopped her "drive-by shooting" critiques, and instead gave employees stretch assignments that allowed them to practice new skills and prove they could go beyond expectations. She even scheduled regular coaching sessions to facilitate their personal leadership growth.

The catalyst for all that change was Denise's new awareness of the way her passion for success had two sides: she needed to balance her energetic appeal to clients against the realities of her team's capabilities and priorities. None of this was easy for Denise, and she was far from perfect. But awareness is about progress, not perfection.

A year later, Denise's agency conducted a new employee survey. It showed that her office improved results by 40 basis points, ranking third out of the twelve offices. Employee churn was reduced by 33 percent. Yes, some employees still went on walkabout, but now it was more likely that they really did have itchy feet than that they wanted to run away from Denise. Through it all, she never stopped selling. That is, Denise remained Denise. She simply learned to lean into her natural style when it served her and add new protocols to help her back off when it didn't.

By becoming a more aware leader, knowing who she was and how she affected others, Denise became a more effective leader.

Why does that type of higher self-awareness contribute to business success? I believe the answer to that question lies in three critical areas: 1) change management, 2) employee engagement, and 3) decision-making. Let's take a closer look at how those three areas work:

Change Management

Any leader in today's fast-moving economy who expects the pace of change to slow is likely to be disappointed. In fact, businesses should embrace change. Without it, organizations would lose their competitive edge and fail to meet the needs of what most hope will be a growing base of loyal customers. Most companies recognize the need to respond to changing consumer needs, and to create new products and services. The typical problem companies face is not that they fail to change, but that they fail to *manage* change.

Organizations that fail to manage change are typically plagued by protracted transitions and increased costs. Just think of:

- Blockbuster, which was crushed by Netflix
- Motorola, which got outmaneuvered by smartphones
- Sears, which lost immense market share to aggressive discount stores such as Walmart and Target
- Yahoo, which fell asleep when Google was inventing and making numerous smart moves

How does self-awareness help leaders manage that sort of change more effectively?

Any change that takes place within an organization is an amalgamation of changes made by individuals. So, to find out how organizations best rise to the challenge of change, we must first ask how individuals best rise to that challenge. The people who make up any organization are best able to implement changes when they are *ready* for change.

In June 2007, researchers at the Air Force Institute of Technology and Auburn University studied a multinational corporation's efforts to create readiness for large-scale change.[5] Researchers identified five themes that indicate a manager's readiness for change: 1) confidence in one's ability to make the proposed change, 2) confidence that the change will benefit oneself personally, 3) recognition that the organization's leadership supports the change, 4) confidence that the change will lead to long-term organizational benefits, and 5) recognition of the need for change. They discovered that a leader's credibility and emotional intelligence affect an organization's change-readiness. Leaders with more self-awareness are aware of the way their behavior impacts others and are therefore better able to project credibility. Leaders who are more self-aware are also more aware of their emotional states, and therefore better able to manage interpersonal relationships and social dynamics.

The rate of change in business is increasing so fast that leaders may believe they have less time to spend on self-awareness. In reality, self-awareness is more critical than ever for leaders to keep up with the pace of change.

Employee Engagement

Self-aware leaders tend to have a better handle on managing their self-esteem as well as recognizing the self-esteem needs of others. This in turn affects their ability to create an environment in which all the members of an organization feel the importance of their contributions. It turns out that increased opportunities to experience self-esteem in connection with an organization translate into increased productivity.

In a 2004 report in the *Journal of Management*, Jon L. Pierce and Donald R. Gardner reviewed a decade of research on self-esteem formed around work and organizational experiences, and its role in employee motivation, attitudes, and behaviors.[6] Researchers observed that employees had greater experiences of self-esteem when organizations sent signals to them about their worth and created opportunities for them to build success. Employees who felt greater self-esteem in relation to work experienced greater job satisfaction, motivation, and organizational commitment. They were also more likely to go above and beyond the basic requirements of their jobs.

It is important for leaders to be aware of what such findings say about them. Their own self-esteem impacts their behavior toward those who work for them, which in turn impacts the self-esteem of those people, which in turn impacts the effectiveness of their entire organization. So it is that organizational self-esteem helps companies maintain a competitive edge.

As a leader, the way you feel about yourself transfers to your organization. This redirection of feelings from you to others can affect change initiatives.

Decision-Making

We know that good leaders make good decisions, but how do they do that? Leaders make the most effective decisions when: 1) they don't let their emotions take over, 2) they reduce their attention to personal bias, and 3) they effectively communicate the risks and benefits of decisions when talking to those whose trust they need. If you are not aware of the way your internal motivations can affect the above three things, then your ability to make quality decisions is impaired.

A study by Takashi Nakao et al. at Nagoya University, Japan and researchers at Hiroshima University has revealed the power of self-awareness to increase the efficiency of decision-making. Researchers prompted students with random pairings of job titles and asked them to choose which of the two occupations they thought they could do better.[7] The researchers used an EEG (electroencephalogram) to measure the students' brain activity in areas associated with conflict in decision-making. Test subjects showed more brain activity, or more conflict, as well as a slower reaction time, when choosing between two job options they found equally attractive. Researchers then stimulated the students' self-awareness by asking them to decide whether various adjectives described them. They then ran the job-choice test again. The students whose self-awareness had been raised showed significantly less conflict and made faster choices than the control groups.

Nakao's research did not say anything about the quality of the students' decision-making. Let's explore that in another arena: medical practice and physicians. In a 2004 review of research on medical errors published in the *Annals of Family Medicine*, Dr. Francesc Borrell-Carrió and Dr. Ronald M. Epstein found that "physicians feel the sensation of making a mistake because of the interference of emotional elements."[8] They proposed helping physicians become more aware of the effect of emotional stressors on their decisions. They concluded that doctors who cultivate emotional self-awareness are likely to function better at making decisions in clinical situations.

Research suggests that self-awareness can increase the speed of your decision-making while also reducing the possibility of emotions getting the better of you.

We all go into every decision with certain biases. Bias is part of being human. The problem in decision-making is not so much that we are biased, but that we are unaware of it. In a 2002 Stanford University review of three studies on objectivity and bias, Emily Pronin, Daniel Lin, and Lee Ross concluded that we are generally more likely to see bias in others than we do in ourselves.[9] We assume that we are more likely than others to see the world as it really is.

If we want to reduce the potential pitfalls of drawing conclusions based on false assumptions, we must start by admitting to ourselves that we do have biases, learning what they are, and opening ourselves to information that may contradict our previously held beliefs.

Effective leaders are perceived as trustworthy. This makes it easy for them to develop relationships with others who support their decisions. Trustworthiness is a function of having a strong personal identity. You can only fully develop a personal identity if you're aware of the beliefs, qualities, and behaviors you bring to the table, when each of them serves you, and when they do not.

Without awareness of our biases, we risk making decisions supported by faulty foundations.

If we look at infamous business scandals, such as those involving Enron, Lehman Brothers, or AIG, most of them involved betrayals of trust on a grand scale. These failures arose out of deceptions ranging from managerial opportunism to creative accounting to outright financial crimes. One thing they all have in common is that in each instance the original sin was the same: self-deception. The roots of self-deception seem to lie in the mind's ability to allay anxiety by distorting self-awareness.

In *Being Wrong: Adventures in the Margin of Error*, journalist Kathryn Schulz lays a case that leaders would benefit from not only admitting but also embracing their fallibility.[10] She points out that we all have a tendency to fear being wrong, but that when we let fear take over, then lying to ourselves is not far behind. Self-deception can lead to problems in our personal lives. In politics, it can lead to war. In business, it can ruin companies, hurting both employees and customers.

We cannot get to know and grow our true selves until we first admit to ourselves that we are born mistake-makers. In the course of any day we will miss the point of conversations, take somebody the wrong way, remember things that never happened, and make false assumptions. We see other people do those things all the time, but we often fail to see them in ourselves. When we begin to accept failure as an integral part of being human, we open ourselves to a wider range of options: to learn from our mistakes, to benefit from the counsel of others, to grow, to change, and in so doing to earn the trust we must have if we are to lead.

When we embrace our fallibility, we free ourselves to become more aware of our motivations, which allows us to make clearer choices about right and wrong. We are actually in a position to better remember our ethical duties, to others and to ourselves.

Leaders earn the trust of others by first engaging in the kind of self-awareness that allows them to admit to themselves that they are not perfect.

In the contemporary business world, much is demanded of you that can threaten your success, your employees' success, and your organization's success. It behooves you to recognize that it is not possible for anyone to be a perfect decision-maker. Internal conflicts, fears, and biases can lead us to delay important decisions, make choices based on mistaken assumptions, or make overconfident predictions. Through self-awareness, we make better-informed decisions in which risk is nothing more or less than a necessary part of change. The aware leader accepts the potential for failure as simply another step on the road to success.

A WORD TO THE AWARE LEADER:

Rumi said, "Yesterday I was clever and I tried to change the world. Today I'm wise and I'm trying to change myself."

TWO

ON A NEED-TO-KNOW BASIS

The One and Only You

"The world is run by those who show up." So goes the wisdom of Robert A. Johnson, renowned Jungian analyst, author, and lecturer on the role of inner transformation in success. But showing up is harder than it sounds. A leader who "shows up" does much more than drag his body to the office. "Showing up" at its most effective requires you to bring all of your genuine self to the present moment. It requires being authentic in this moment, and this one, and now this one. The key to being fully present is self-awareness.

> *No leadership competency is more important than self-awareness.*

If you are like most business leaders, the focus of your personal development has been on increasing your knowledge, experience, and skills. Out of the sixty billion dollars that companies and individuals spend on leadership development each year, most of that goes to skill development. Although that's a good investment, it's not what will send you ahead of the pack. If you want to be the most aware leader you can be, what you really need to understand are your personal behavior, style, and preferences.

The challenge that arises when leadership development focuses on knowledge, experience, and skills is that we cannot apply those things to the best effect unless we also know our behaviors, styles, and preferences. If we don't discover our personal qualities and learn how to apply them effectively, the downsides of those qualities can turn on us and diminish our other hard-won competencies.

Think about a person you know who is a great strategic thinker but who also has poor interpersonal skills. Have you noticed how hard it is for that person to successfully execute even their most amazing strategies because they fail to elicit the support of others? Experience has taught me one crucial thing about such people: they are not self-reflective. If they were, they would not tear down their own hard work with their ineffective style. Here's what that should tell you: if you have not been spending time and effort getting to know yourself, you could very well be in a similar boat to the person you just thought of.

Most of us spend little time on self-awareness. In fact, we are habit-bound. In a 2005 article in the *Journal of Personality and Social Psychology*, Wood, Tam, and Witt put it this way: "Daily life is characterized by repetition...a full 47% of people's daily activities are enacted almost daily and usually in the same location. The consistency of everyday life establishes habits, or behavioral dispositions to repeat well-practiced actions given recurring circumstances"[11]

A large part of our days is spent on automatic pilot, while we remain largely unconscious.

When I talk about developing self-awareness I'm not talking about undergoing the typical evaluations employers have likely given you in the past, in which you answer a list of pat questions and then have a chat about your strengths and weaknesses. That's an oversimplification of the complexity of you. Finding out the kind of leader you are is not something you can discover from an annual review, or a quick listing of what you like about yourself and what you don't.

I'm talking about digging deep to discover the underlying things that make you tick, how those inner motivators express themselves in your behavior, how that behavior changes whether you are in your element or under stress, and how all of this impacts others. I'm talking about coming to know your personal attributes so well that you can learn when they help you and when they hinder you. I'm talking about knowing how to draft your total self into service—even the parts of yourself you never thought you had a use for—to help you express your values and move toward your objectives in life.

"You need to know yourself from the inside— the person you think you are, your hopes, dreams, aspirations, values, fears, and belief about how to get along, get ahead, and find meaning. " — Dan McAdams[12]

I ask you to begin your journey to self-discovery by recognizing your uniqueness. Sure, we all have a lot in common: we all work and play, love and lose, live and die. But within those common experiences, we are each so distinctive it boggles the mind. Every year I assess hundreds of executives, and I assess 94 attributes for each of them. If you do a factorial of 94, you'll learn that, based on this assessment, there are 1.087×10^{146} possible types of people. You're one of them. Getting to know *you* begins by accepting the possibility that you can make a contribution to the world which nobody else can make. The best way to tap into that is to explore yourself. Not just the things you want to know, or the things you hope are true, but all of it.

Embrace Your Existential Crisis

At some point in life, almost all of us encounter problems that our personal philosophies cannot resolve. This happens when we witness events that challenge our worldview, listen to opinions contrary to our own, or engage in new experiences that force us to question our assumptions. This is not to be avoided but embraced, because it is in facing those challenging moments of existential angst that we encounter our authentic selves.

Try the following exercise in mindfulness to learn about your uniqueness:

MINDFUL MOMENT #1
GETTING TO KNOW YOU

Find a comfortable spot without distractions. Close your eyes and take a few deep breaths. When you're ready, send yourself back into these three parts of your life, in turn:

From birth to college: For five minutes, recall some of the experiences, events, and people that had the most influence on you during this period of your life. Don't worry about thinking up the "right" memories, just relax and ponder the first ones that come to mind.

From college graduation to your early career: For five minutes, recall some of the experiences, events, and people that had the most influence on you during this period of your life. Again, just let whatever comes up be your guide.

From the last ten years to now: For five minutes, recall some of the experiences, events, and people that had, or are having, the most influence on who you are today. Be honest with yourself. Nobody is judging your answers, and the idea is to get to the real you.

Now, close your eyes one more time as you ask yourself the following two questions:

1. How did the above memories shape who you are and how you lead?

2. How is your collection of experiences and responses unique to you?

I have many more mindfulness exercises where this one came from, and I'll share them throughout the book.

Although you might know other people who can relate to your experiences and choices, you alone have lived the story of you. That story makes you the leader you are now. How will you get to know that leader inside and out? First, you need to know how your life story translates into the values, the personal style, and the behaviors that define you.

The Forgotten Side of You

Many leaders have tried to go on the journey to self-knowledge before, but have unwittingly used it to perpetuate a campaign of misinformation within their own heads. Sometimes we're tempted to ignore information that makes us uncomfortable because it suggests we might not be the infallible leaders we want to believe we are. Other times we're tempted to pursue only the information that allows us to beat ourselves up for our flaws. We might believe dwelling on our flaws springs from humility, but it's actually a defeatist attitude in which we let ourselves off the hook by telling stories about how failure is ingrained in us and we can't help it.

The way we leverage our knowledge, experience, and skills is influenced by the way our inner selves have developed from our relationships with early authority figures, significant life experiences, examples set by other executives, implicit learning, and formal leadership training. As poet Walt Whitman wrote, "I am large, I contain multitudes." Getting to know the multitudes within you will help you align your knowledge, experience, and skills with your personal qualities so that you can integrate all your capabilities for success.

Every one of the multitudes within you has leadership potential. You simply need to know when a characteristic serves you and when it doesn't. A self-confident, aggressive leader with high expectations may be highly successful in building a business. On the other hand, others may view that leader as arrogant and insensitive. A caring, supportive leader may be appreciated for showing empathy for people, but may find it difficult to take a firm stand and act assertively.

It's often when we're under stress that our leadership characteristics turn on us, when one of our best qualities can seem like one of our worst. I remember when Tim, a hospital CEO who consulted with me, was seeking approval for a 600-million-dollar bond and really feeling the pressure. He was an assertive guy, which had helped him get this far, but now it was costing him points with his board. He called me and explained, "I'm getting feedback that I'm coming on too strong, the New Yorker side of me coming out in the Midwest. But man, that's just who I am!"

I could certainly see that side of him, but nobody is just one thing. I reminded him of a personal story he had shared with me. In fact, this story has become part of his mythos at the company. He was on his way to a meeting one day when he walked into the cafeteria, saw two ladies from the janitorial staff eating lunch, and sat to talk with them. One of them was talking about a death in her family. He took her hand and listened intently and demonstrated quiet empathy. "Let me ask you, Tim," I said. "Which person are you, the blustery guy or the compassionate guy?"

The answer is: he's both.

We each have many personas. Leadership is about bringing out the persona appropriate to the moment. "You were there for that person," I told him. "You had the right message for that person. You were fully present with that person. Can you bring that other self into some of the more public situations you deal with, by planning ahead and knowing who you're talking to?"

That's when he pointed out the problem many leaders have with wearing different hats: "But it's so damn hard. I'm always rushing to get there. I just don't have time for that."

I challenged him on that one, as I would any leader committed to self-awareness. When we know ourselves, we stop seeing our personal challenges as unsolvable problems and instead open ourselves to choices. In that vein, I suggested, "So is it possible that you can schedule the time you need to get yourself in the right mindset before these meetings, since you're looking for a 600-million-dollar bond approval and it's very important?"

He immediately saw the value in allowing self-awareness to dictate a new choice in his scheduling. We were on the phone, and he said, "When we hang up I'm talking to my assistant, and I'm going to have her make sure I always have thirty minutes to myself before I go to those meetings."

He had been telling only one story about himself: *I'm a bold, brash New Yorker. This is who I am.* Now he added a new story to tell: *I'm also the kind, compassionate listener from the cafeteria.* Both are part of the total person that is Tim, and together they got the bond approved.

As leaders, we need to set aside judgment and introduce ourselves to all of our selves. We need to acknowledge that talented people sometimes fail. Despite knowledge, experience, and skills, a variety of personality factors can limit our ability to perform consistently. What often arrives during these difficult times is problematic behavior in our relationships.

Your relationships, both with yourself and with others, provide a context that defines your workplace. The qualities that can derail you usually reflect distorted beliefs about yourself, about how others will treat you, and about the best means to achieve your goals. Acting on false assumptions about who you are can negatively influence your career and your satisfaction with life. When you embrace all that you are, you give yourself options to make new choices. The more choices you have, the greater your opportunities for success.

Under the Iceberg

I was on a call with the president of a large nonprofit when she told me she had recently turned fifty and was finally accepting her introversion. For forty-some years she had viewed her introversion as a negative for which she must compensate. The good news was that she had developed social intention skills to help her succeed. The bad news was that at first her decision to "accept herself" sounded a lot more like "giving up on herself." She was still holding on to the self-perception that her introversion was undesirable. She was heartened when I shared a 2012 article titled "The Upside of Being an Introvert," by Bryan Walsh, in which he debunked myths about introverts, such as being shy or lacking leadership, and espoused their positive qualities, such as intense focus, excellent listening skills, and careful risk assessment.[13]

We can know ourselves on many levels, some deep, some superficial. As large as an iceberg might appear, more than seventy-five percent of it lies hidden beneath the surface. It is a thing of beauty, but when nobody considers what's underneath, it can sink a ship. Think of yourself as an iceberg: so much beneath the surface is strong and beautiful, if only you look for it, but if you don't pay attention to what's underneath, there is much you can destroy.

TRUE SELF-AWARENESS ASKS YOU TO DEVELOP:

- greater knowledge of your values
- broader perception about how you behave as a leader
- increased knowledge about what triggers you in negative and positive ways
- expanded openness to seeing life in a new way

Let's explore an idea that I suggest you bookmark and revisit again and again as you pursue each milestone on your leadership journey:

AFTER THE MIRACLE HAPPENS

Get out a pad and pen. Now pause and imagine that you go to sleep tonight and while you are sleeping a miracle happens: all of the advances you hope to make in your life as a business leader, community member, parent, spouse, friend, or family member have taken place. Now write down the answers to the following questions, using as much detail as you can.

1. When you wake up in the morning, what is the first thing you notice you are doing that tells you the miracle has happened?

2. What do you notice that is different around your home or office?
3. Who is with you?
4. What is that person saying?
5. What experiences have you had during your life that advanced you to this moment?
6. What are your spouse, children, family, friends, or colleagues saying about you?
7. What are you hearing about what kind of leader you are?
8. What else do you notice?

Now read your answers aloud. This is your personal vision statement.

The above exercise uses your imagination to project you into a future that you have the power to create. Your brain recognizes a virtual reality that you can make an actual reality. To get there, your next step is to deduce the following: "I *can* be the person described in my answer to The Miracle Question. It requires that I not only gain knowledge, create experiences, and add skills, but also that I understand and augment my behavior, styles, and preferences."

Once you accept that, then you will be ready to answer two more questions:

1. What are you doing in your life daily that is moving you toward the above miracle morning?
1. What are you doing in your life daily that is moving you away from it?

The Observing Self

It might be easier to answer the above two questions if you first develop a critical skill: self-observation. Self-observation is neither self-criticism nor self-absorption. In self-observation, we need to be aware of, and be open to, our thoughts, emotions, and moods—and to see them for what they are. Think of it as watching yourself from behind a video camera.

"To self-observe means to not become attached to or to identify with any content of our experience, but to watch alertly, openly, passively." – James Flaherty[2]14

Self-observation is the way you get to know the *multitudes* within you that Walt Whitman talked about. When I use the term *multitudes*, I mean we each exist simultaneously at many levels of consciousness. The multitudes that inhabit us, with their variety of beliefs, attitudes, and feelings, contradict our limited idea of who we are, and sometimes even contradict one another. While this might sound confusing at first, self-observation can help you make sense of the apparent contradictions within you and make them work together for your benefit.

We might say that our many different levels of consciousness exist at different frequencies, like the many channels on Sirius XM. When we react to a stressful situation by tuning in to one channel, we may be unaware that we can choose to switch to a different channel.

Not quite sure what I mean? Try this:

Imagine the way you interact with your spouse when he/she does something that triggers you to become angry. Now imagine when you are at work and your boss does the same thing. Notice how your reaction is different? You can actually train yourself to have those alternate channels at your disposal when you need them. But first you must become aware that they're inside you and that you have access to them. Then you must learn to observe yourself, so you know when you need them.

With practice, anyone can develop an observing self. The observing self uses the tools of both detachment (the microscope of the scientist) and compassion (the first-aid kit of the friend). The observer stands outside of our selves and our lives, objectively noting what is experienced so it can understand the reality of the situation. As you develop the observing self, it becomes your own observatory, where part of you can regularly sit and calmly stare into the multitude of others that make up you, learning to notice and name them all.

The ability to observe yourself objectively and compassionately is the single most important skill you need to achieve your personal vision.

The observing self is different from your thinking self, emotional self, or physical self. It's the side of you that notices all your other selves without judging them. Not that judgment is never called for—we're all susceptible to mistakes now and then, and sometimes we have to call on our conscience to prevent those mistakes or make amends for them—it's just that this sort of judgment is not the job of your observing self. Your inner observer is simply conscious of whatever you're thinking, feeling, or doing at any moment. That part of your mind allows you to rationally choose which other self to call to your aid in a challenging situation.

The benefit of this practice is that the mind becomes quiet, allowing us to notice things without the running commentary of a loquacious (chatty) mind. Preoccupation, rumination, distraction, and daydreaming are examples of a loquacious mind. When the mind quiets, the observing self can do its job, which is to help you develop a deeper awareness of who you are.

Know What You Bring to the Table

It's likely you work for an organization that defines effective performance by a list of competencies, a.k.a. "behaviors," which research has shown to be common among high performers. Those competencies describe what we should do and how we should do it. Attributes, a.k.a. "styles and preferences," describe *why* we do what we do. Research has illustrated that our attributes drive our competencies. So, if our styles and preferences influence our behaviors, and our behaviors affect our job performance, then it only follows that getting to know what makes us tick will help us perform at higher levels.

You may already know a bit about what some call your strengths and weaknesses, but that's not the same as knowing yourself. Tom, the blustery banking CEO, knew he tended to blow up, but that was not helping him work with his team. What he needed to make him as effective as possible was to understand the ways in which his underlying attributes facilitated or hindered his performance.

Your attributes have the power to move you either toward or away from your personal vision, at least as much as your knowledge, experience, or skills. Drs. Joyce and Robert Hogan challenged decades of academic tradition to become the first to demonstrate the impact of people's personalities on organizational effectiveness. They founded Hogan Assessments in 1987, pioneering the use of personality assessments to improve workplace performance. Their flagship assessment, the Hogan Personality Inventory, was the first measure of normal personality designed for the business community (as opposed to tests designed to determine psychological disorders). Today, Hogan uses a variety of assessments to help leaders understand their capabilities, challenges, and drivers, so they can develop the self-awareness that makes good leaders great.

As both an executive coach and a certified Hogan Assessments consultant, I've had an opportunity to witness firsthand the way personality attributes impact performance:

A FEW ATTRIBUTES THAT FACILITATE PERFORMANCE, ACCORDING TO HOGAN ASSESSMENTS:15

- composure
- optimism
- stable moods
- initiative

- competitive nature
- energy
- self-confidence
- curiosity
- imagination
- intelligence
- interest in intellectual matters
- strong motivation to learn

A FEW ATTRIBUTES THAT HINDER PERFORMANCE, ACCORDING TO HOGAN ASSESSMENTS:15

- temperamental nature
- irritability
- propensity for emotional outbursts
- assertive self-promotion
- arrogance
- excessive restraint
- reluctance to try new things
- overly sensitive to criticism
- eccentricity
- reluctance to take independent action

If you are missing a few attributes from the first list, or if you have a few attributes from the second—never fear. Many combinations of these attributes exist among us all. Many attributes that facilitate performance are simply the flip side of attributes that can also hinder performance. For example, creativity taken too far can become eccentricity, or a competitive nature dialed up a notch might become arrogance. It depends on the circumstances. The point is, if we do not become aware of our attributes and how they help or hinder us, it won't matter how much effort we put into attaining knowledge, experience, and skills. This critical information allows us to leverage our useful attributes and to mitigate those that don't serve us.

Taking a professional personality assessment, of which Hogan is just one, can benefit you by helping you understand more about your attributes, as well as your core values, goals, and interests. Such assessments measure how you approach work and how you interact with others. They can also help identify your "derailers," which are those adverse behaviors that become your go-to position when you experience stress or boredom. Derailing behaviors can impede work relationships, adversely impact your leadership style, and hinder productivity, all of which can limit your career potential. Identifying derailers can prevent such problems before they arise.

It's important to keep the observing self at the center of it all, witnessing your attributes in action so you can continually hone your self-knowledge. As you develop your self-observational skills, you will empower yourself to make better choices, in your career and all areas of your life.

A WORD TO THE AWARE LEADER:

If you are not investing effort in figuring out who you are and why you behave the way you do, you might be sabotaging your own success without even knowing it.

THREE

YOUR DEFAULT SETTINGS

The Power of a Story

I'm from Texas, and Texans believe storytelling is in our DNA. In the town of George West, The Storytelling Capital of Texas, they hold an annual Storyfest. The Tejas Storytelling Association conducts an annual Texas Liars Contest. But Texans don't have a monopoly on stories. As far back as the days of cave paintings, humans have used stories to make sense of their world, to pass information from generation to generation, and to strengthen community bonds.

> *We experience our world and ourselves within the framework of stories.*

To give you an idea of the value of stories in successful leadership, let me tell you about Peter. Peter was the internal candidate selected to run a global manufacturing company. The board felt he was the best person for the job but had concerns about his occasional outbursts with team members. They asked him to work with a coach. That's where I came in.

One of the first things I did was to seek 360-feedback from Peter's executive team.

When he and I discussed the feedback, I said, "Peter, they're describing you as a Doctor Jekyll and Mr. Hyde. There's this one guy who is unbelievably magnanimous, always there for you. Then there's this other guy who is explosive, who lashes out without warning."

He was not surprised. "Yeah, I'm aware of that."

Although Peter knew he needed to work on his temper, he also felt justified in his anger at the team. He was not in the habit of self-observation. He did not realize that he was not reasoning but reacting. After our talk, he worked on observing himself, noticing when his team triggered him, what his behavior was like when triggered, and the effect it had on his team.

During our next session, we got to the heart of the matter. He told me his story.

"You know what drives me nuts?" he said. "It's the slackers on my team."

"Slackers on your C-level?" I said. "That's a strong word. What makes them slackers?"

We talked a while, but for Peter it boiled down to this: "They should damn well know when they have to kick in and work harder. When I grew up on my grandfather's farm, there were times we had to get up at 5:30 to do chores, and then I had to go to school and come back to do more chores. If the hay needed bailing, we bailed hay, because it had to be done."

"You really have a strong point of view about working hard," I said. "Working hard is a rule for you, a principle people should live by. Do I understand you correctly?"

"Absolutely. People should know the value of hard work."

"Fair enough, but how many people on your team know that it's a rule?" I asked.

He looked perplexed. "I don't know."

I said, "I want you to think about the times that you've let people have it. How many times did it have to do with them not following this rule?"

He thought about it and admitted that it accounted for many of his blow-ups.

I asked him if there were other rules he lived by. There were four and they were strong.

I said, "Think about all the times you've exploded. Do those rules cover every time?"

"Every one." He had the look of someone who had just woken up.

I said, "What do you think would happen if they knew the rules? At a minimum, they would at least know they're breaking them."

He said, "That's an awesome idea. I'm going to write down my rules, and at our next meeting I'm going to tell them, 'These are my four rules, and if you're wondering why I got mad at you before, it's because you broke one of these rules.'"

Would you believe his team loved it? They finally knew where his explosions were coming from. They said, "Why don't we print up the rules and post them?" Today when things get tense, someone says, "Rule Number Four!" or "Rule Number One!" They now have more information about when they need to step up, and they step up. In turn, Peter has calmed down.

Like any human, Peter will never be perfect. He still blows up now and again, but not half as much as before. When he does, both he and his team have a better understanding of why it's happening and how to deal with it, so it doesn't impact their overall performance.

Through the practice of self-observation, Peter discovered the way his personal stories influenced him. Once he noticed that, he also saw that his team came to the table with their own stories. He became aware of how his internal values affected his behaviors and how those behaviors affected others. He did not have to become a different person to achieve change. He just needed to understand himself. Now, instead of reacting unconsciously, he leverages his awareness of his stories and the values they represent, to create results. Once he saw how changing his own perceptions affected his team, he stopped calling them "slackers."

When Our Stories Limit Us

We use stories to highlight pivotal moments in our lives: the moments when we have faced our biggest challenges, when we have succeeded or failed, when we have learned hard lessons or demonstrated the best of ourselves. These stories define us. Think of a story you tell in public or at parties when you want to give people a taste of who you are. What value or belief about yourself does the story represent? Such stories can be powerful, but it's the stories you *don't* tell that tend to have the power to blindside you.

Let's try an experiment. Consider a one-line belief about yourself or about life in general that you silently tell yourself on a regular basis. If you can't think of one, here are a few possibilities:

OH, THE STORIES WE TELL OURSELVES!

- People say I'm moody, but I'm just passionate.
- I've learned the hard way: always be alert for signs of deception.
- Don't make a mistake or people will criticize you.
- Keeping people at a distance prevents getting hurt.
- My agenda is the right one, but it's a waste of time trying to convince people.
- What is life without risk? Boring.
- I'm creative, but people don't get me.
- If you want it done right, do it my way.
- There's nothing wrong with telling a boss what they want to hear.
- I get on people's nerves because I talk too much.
- I know the value of hard work better than most people.

Now that you have a belief in mind, think of the last time you listened to it. How did you apply this internal narrative to the outer circumstance you were facing? What does this story say about you? This sort of one-liner may not sound like much of a story to you, but if you dig a little deeper you'll find that it's shorthand for an important memory from your life. To get at that memory, try asking yourself: *What was the first experience that taught me the truth behind this idea?* The memory might come to you in fragments. That's okay; don't rush yourself. My words will be waiting here for you when you're done...

Got it? Okay, that's your story, one of the formative memories that cause you to think of your life a certain way, informing your values and motivating your actions. Such stories can carry you to success like *The Little Engine That Could* or they can completely derail you. If you're not conscious of the way these stories affect your inner engine, you have little choice about which way the train goes.

Memories create subconscious stories to help you make unfamiliar new experiences feel familiar: "Oh, this is like that time when..." Categorizing new experiences according to your list of stories helps you perform tasks without having to constantly figure things out. Sometimes this autonomic process facilitates success. Other times it can limit your choices as a leader.

I carry around a few stories that I used to unconsciously allow to limit me. For forty years I carried a strong self-perception that I was unattractive. I disliked mirrors, having my picture taken, or shopping for clothes—because I believed nothing could solve my problem. I craved constant validation from others about my appearance, but I never believed it when somebody told me I looked good. My insecurity put a strain on personal relationships and made it hard for me to step out front and be noticed in my profession.

On my thirtieth birthday, I took drastic action. I went to a hair salon for a body wave because I was sure my hair was too straight and fine. I thought if I had hair like the guys in *Esquire*, I might be less embarrassed by my looks. It only made things worse: my colleagues roared with laughter when I walked into the office with my new hair, which was more curly like a clown's than it was wavy like an *Esquire* model's. Instead of recognizing that they thought I looked fine *before* the perm, I saw the experience as further proof that I was hard on the eyes. My *story* was stronger than the evidence.

I had never bothered to learn the real story behind my story, so I had no options to deal with it. On my journey to become an aware leader, I finally traced my story back to an awkward adolescence. I had spent my self-conscious high-school years as the butt of jokes about being bucktoothed, clumsy, and wearing high-water pants because I was so gangly. At Baylor University, my roommate, Jeff, clued me in on an embarrassing but important truth: I dressed so differently from others that it went beyond personal style to social awkwardness.

As time went on, I grew into my lanky frame and my teeth, became more athletic and graceful, and listened to the advice of trusted friends on appropriate dress. Unfortunately, I also continued listening to the voices in my head, which still picked on the guy I used to be.

I will never silence the voices of my past, but now that I know where they come from, they no longer have the power to shape my opinion of myself.

When our stories define us in a limiting way, we often talk ourselves into jams or talk ourselves out of opportunities simply because we're ruled by our old familiar script. We doubt people's good intentions and feel validated when they disappoint us. We avoid situations because we imagine potential embarrassment. We put off decisions for fear of criticism. We remain privately irritated about situations but hide our frustration lest we confirm the bad opinion of others. We believe we deserve special treatment but are sure we won't get it. We maintain high standards for ourselves in hopes of making everyone okay with us, but rail at the unfairness when others don't live by the same high standards. We're eager to please and careful not to contradict those we work for.

Once we recognize our stories, and the way we reinforce them by giving them undue attention, we have the power to rewrite them. As real as they seem, they're not. They're illusions based on memories of a time that no longer exists. They prevent us from seeing the present as it really is. Memories only have the power we give them.

Getting Stuck in a Default Story

Speaking of stories, have you heard this one that author David Foster Wallace told during his famous 2005 commencement speech at Kenyon College?

> *There are these two young fish swimming along, and they happen to meet an older fish swimming the other way, who nods at them and says, "Morning, boys, how's the water?" And the two young fish swim on for a bit, and then eventually one of them looks over at the other and goes, "What the hell is water?"*
>
> *If at this moment, you're worried that I plan to present myself here as the wise old fish explaining what water is to you younger fish, please don't be. I am not the wise old fish. The immediate point of the fish story is that the most obvious, ubiquitous, important realities are often the ones that are the hardest to see and talk about.*
> — David Foster Wallace[16]

Most of us walk around feeling pretty sure that the world we experience is real. We can see, hear, touch, taste, and smell it. We pick up objects and feel their weight. Sometimes, if we pick up those objects, drop them, or trip over them, we can hurt ourselves. It seems undeniable that a tangible physical world is out there, independent and apart from us.

All is not as it seems.

First, it turns out that the apparently solid book or e-reader you're holding is, in fact, not solid. With the advent of quantum theory, scientists discovered that all matter is mostly empty space. When we look closely at the tiny electrons, protons, neutrons, and other subatomic particles whirling through that empty space, we discover that they, too, are far from solid.

Second, it's easy to think that the colors we see, sounds we hear, foods we taste, and sensations we feel are direct representations of reality. In this, too, we're often mistaken. Sensory perception is limited. Our eyes don't see the full light spectrum, our ears don't hear the full sound spectrum, and all of our senses can be fooled. What's more, all we know of the world are images produced in the mind, which is influenced by opinion, emotion, and subjective experience.

We think we see a tree exactly as it is, but nobody else will ever know precisely what you see when you see a tree...and you will never know precisely what they see.

Your brain is shaped by early experiences. In fact, studies show that your brain may also be genetically shaped by your ancestors' experiences. In a group of studies published in *Discover* in 2013, molecular biologist and geneticist Moshe Szyf and neurobiologist Michael Meaney, both of Montreal's McGill University, discovered that traumatic experiences can cause permanent changes in DNA, changes that get passed on to later generations.[17] Their studies indicated that if you suffer poverty, abuse, or neglect as a child, it can scar your genes for life, causing a predisposition to depression and anxiety. What's more, if your parents or grandparents suffered such genetic scars, they likely passed them on to you.

By adulthood, your mind is programmed with many default settings. When you're aware of those defaults, you maintain more choice in your attitudes and behaviors.

In computer science, a default setting refers to a preset value that is automatically assigned to a software application, computer program, or electronic device, which stays in place unless a user changes it. Defaults are intended to make a device easier to use "right out of the box." Programmers select a common setting based on what they believe most users will want.

You can choose to change some of a computer's default settings—your browser for example—to better meet your distinct needs. But studies have shown that once a set of default settings are assigned, they increase the likelihood that the user will choose to use the device only in the ways suggested by the settings. This is known as the "default effect."

Like a computer, you have default settings. Those are your go-to actions, based on a preset list of choices, which are suggested by the stories you've created to define your life.

Luckily, like a computer owner, you have the power to adjust your default settings. This won't require you to change your stories. Your stories and the resulting default settings will always be yours. The trick is to adjust those settings to suit your needs. To do that you first need to know, and acknowledge, your stories and how they affect your choices.

The Story Holly Never Told

We each have a narrative identity, an internal life story in which we integrate memories of our past with imaginings about our future to give ourselves a sense of purpose. In "Narrative Identity," a 2013 article published in *Current Directions in Psychological Science*, psychologists Dan P. McAdams and Kate C. McLean made the case that people who derive redemptive meaning from adversity tend to enjoy higher levels of well-being, creativity, and productivity.[18]

I'll never forget how one of my clients completely changed her life by unearthing a buried story. Holly is now a senior leader for a government behavioral health organization. The board initially passed Holly over because they found an external candidate who seemed stronger. The external hire did not work out, so Holly was made an interim executive, with an opportunity to earn that role on a permanent basis. The board brought me in to coach her in hopes of increasing her chance at success.

As usual with a new client, I sought 360-feedback on Holly. Colleagues described her as passionate, patient-centric, prudent, trustworthy, detailed, and hardworking. Hand-in-hand with that, though, they also described her as stressed, a micromanager, and a poor listener. They said everything was urgent with Holly, which created a tense work environment.

What they did not know was Holly's story.

I gave her an assessment, which included a scale called "good attachment." If someone scores low on "good attachment," that usually indicates a difficult childhood. Mind you, I don't put leaders on a psychiatrist's couch and ask them to dig deep into childhood experiences. What I do is assist them in making connections to jump-start self-awareness. With Holly, our goal was to uncover her story so she could see how it connected to the default settings that drove her. I've found that if you name a story, you can make new choices about how to react when it comes up.

During our first session, Holly and I talked through the Mindful Moment exercise I asked you to do in Chapter Two, in which you divided your life into thirds. I was interested in the key life experiences that shaped the person she had become. The scores on her leadership assessment told me there must be an intense story in there somewhere, but it was her choice to find it.

When she initially told me about the first twenty years of her life, it sounded like she had a happy childhood. Then, in the midst of her tales of loving times with family, playing with friends, and doing well in school, she grew quiet. I took that opportunity to explain that her low score on "good attachment" suggested she might not be telling the whole story.

"You don't have to talk about it," I reassured her, "but I want you to understand that whatever trauma happened back then, it seems to be affecting your performance now."

She leaned forward and lowered her voice, "I'm going to tell you something, and you'll be the second person ever in my life that I've told."

Holly unfolded an incredible story. She came from a family of religious fundamentalists with rigid rules. Her father turned violent whenever she broke a rule. Her mother lacked compassion. Holly had no memory of her mom ever hugging her or saying "I love you." But Holly's darkest secret was this: "From the age of four to eight, I was molested by my brother-in-law."

Those experiences contributed to Holly's default settings, everything from compassion for patients, to attention to rules, to excessive vigilance in trying to please the new stand-ins for her parents: her bosses.

The problem was, she believed she must hide her secret or risk someone discovering she was flawed. Her mind was tuned to Radio Doom and Gloom, broadcasting gloom from the past that made her dissatisfied with the present and fearful of doom in the future.

The good news was that Holly didn't need to change the facts of her life. She just needed to become aware of her story so she could reframe it. Her story need not be about a failure who feared getting found out. It could be about a resilient woman who thrived against the odds.

Here's the part of her story I haven't told you yet: Holly had delayed college for years because she feared failure, but she landed a job in a bank where she worked hard, got promoted, and became the only non-degreed vice president. That taste of success, combined with a desire to serve, nudged her to go to college to create a more meaningful career. At twenty-eight, with her husband's support, she earned a nursing degree. Her first job out of college was at a women's psychiatric hospital, where she discovered that a majority of the patients had been sexually abused. This tugged at her. She was a fellow survivor who wanted to help. Her default setting of vigilance was not all bad: it led to promotions.

Still, Holly's secret story was burning a hole inside her. So she increased her vigilance, until it backfired: holding her back from the confidence and ease with others that she needed to convince the board to promote her. She had to reconsider her story or she was going to fail.

After Holly became aware of her story and how it was limiting her, I watched her begin to make new choices about who she wanted to be in the world. She acknowledged that holding so tightly to her secret was feeding her habit of excessive vigilance. She chose to tell her husband and a handful of trusted confidants about her childhood sexual abuse. She accepted that she could not change her emotionally stunted mother, who now had Alzheimer's, but she chose to start hugging her mom and telling her mom she loved her. Her mother was thrilled, and even hugged her back. Holly made the choice to treat herself to the love she had missed.

As for the hypervigilance, that will always be a challenge for Holly. But now that she knows why, she gets to practice compassion with herself. She offers herself understanding and chooses not to react to the past voices of her angry father and cold mother.

Holly is now a fulfilled, less stressed-out, more successful leader whom others love to follow. She is no longer an interim executive. The board has chosen her for the long haul.

Naming Your Default Settings

In *The Monk Who Sold His Ferrari*, author Robin Sharma tells us: "The mind is a wonderful servant, but a terrible master."[19] Without an understanding of our default settings, the mind can push us around. Most of us are not conscious of the impact our default settings have.

Sure, your brain might detect patterns: someone squints at you funny at meetings and you decide he's judging you, an argument with a peer confirms your fear that you're a people-repelling troll, or a boss's dismissive attitude convinces you that your friends are right about the soulless corporate world. Life is full of chaos, and it's tempting to rely on default stories to deal with that, but conclusions based on subconscious fears are not always true or relevant. When you let your mind whir incessantly, that can lead you into mental traps that prevent you from being present. It is only when you're fully present that you can see things as they are and respond as your most effective self. This is the first step to being the leader you want to be.

Don't worry about trying to shut off Radio Station Doom and Gloom. There is no "off" switch for your default settings. However, you can choose to turn the volume down so the noise stops distracting you from the opportunities before you.

When we learn to recognize our default settings, we create more choices in our lives about what we focus on and how we show up.

If you want more choices in life, it helps to know how your default settings influence the way you choose to see things. I'm not necessarily recommending psychotherapy (though that can be helpful). What I'm recommending is that you strengthen your observing self: your ability to see yourself and the world around you with nonjudgmental detachment. How do you get there? The observing self is like a muscle; it grows stronger through practice.

What does your observing self need to practice? Mindfulness.

Mindfulness to naturally arising thoughts, feelings, and sensations helps you identify which thoughts, feelings, and sensations are not aiding you. By impartially observing them as they pass, the first lesson you internalize is that they *do pass*. The more accustomed you become to that idea, the less you will find yourself a victim of your emotions, and the more you will maintain the ability to make rational choices in the moment.

The goal is to experience with awareness whatever is happening in the moment. Noticing what goes on in your mind without reacting is a practice that will help you overcome the automatic fight or flight response that can get us in trouble in the stressful world of leadership.

When you become aware of your experience, the next step is to name your thoughts about the experience. When your thoughts have a name, you have the power to choose how you think about them. You can move from "that thought is *me*," to "that is only a thought *about* me."

How do you name your thoughts? Let's go back to Holly. In the past, her thoughts might have gone something like this: "You're a person who screws up. Your dad told you that, other people told you that, and you've seen it. You'd better watch out because you're a screw-up." Her story, or default setting, sent her thoughts spiraling from recognizing the potential to make a mistake to naming herself "a screw-up." She had even roped in her sexual abuse story as proof: *if you had only done something different, that wouldn't have happened.* That's powerful.

Once she knew her story, she had the power to name it. Now when she feels panic rising, she tells herself something like, "That's *the zealot father thing*. Don't let it push you into overdrive, thinking you have to fix everything. Nobody's going to beat you up."

> *Once she named her demon, she could detach*
> *from it. She was free to choose a new story.*

It was not I who helped Holly achieve a new vision of her story. Holly did that for herself. My only role was to support her, the way Dr. Gadol had supported me. He helped me make a connection between my tendency to ruminate on my failures and my desire to please my father. Now, anytime I start ruminating, I just name the thought: "That's just *the dad thing.*" This practice allows me to remember who I am and snap out of it.

Once you name your default story, you don't have to keep reliving it. It's all there, in the name. It doesn't matter what you name it: "crummy upbringing" will do. The idea is to remind yourself that it's just a story, not who you are. You have the power to tell a new story, right now.

This is not easy. There have been times on my journey when I would make a mistake and all of it would come back. I would forget to tell myself that it was just *the dad thing*, and I would find myself back in the struggle because I couldn't let it go. Becoming an aware leader is not a destination, it's a journey. The important thing is not that you walk a perfect path, but that you don't give up. Sooner or later, I always remember my power to choose. The more I do it, the easier it gets. If you practice, it will get easier for you too.

A WORD TO THE AWARE LEADER:

It is unimaginably hard to do this, to stay conscious and alive,
day in and day out.

—David Foster Wallace

FOUR

WAKE YOURSELF UP

How Do We Change Our Stories?

Leaders need to be awake to the possibilities of the moment, unclouded by stories from the past or fears about the future. Leaders also need to be aware of the choices available within them. They cannot act on those choices if they're weighed down by a false sense of self or lack of self-awareness.

Now that you know your story, how will you reframe it so it serves you? Now that you know your default settings, how will you ensure they don't take over your actions? Now that you're ready to make conscious choices, how will you stay awake to the evolving story of you?

You will always be you, but the way you tell The Story of You is always open for revision. The key is to stay mindful to what lies within you and before you at every moment.

The following are a few reminders I offer clients, and also practice myself, to stay awake to the possibility of writing my own story instead of letting my story write me:

1. **Pay Attention**: Observe yourself and name your thoughts so you can start identifying your stories. I've found truth in the adage that whatever we give our attention to grows. So our goal is to give ourselves only the most useful stories to pay attention to. This calls on us to shift our thinking, to retrain our brains to create new stories. Only by acknowledging your old stories can you consider what it would take to let go of the chapters that aren't serving you. You will discover that although those old stories might keep playing in the back of your mind, you always have the power to write new ones.

2. **Create Intention**: In the John Lennon song "Mind Games," he sings about searching for the grail, a metaphor for our purpose in life. To find this grail, Lennon exhorts us to raise our consciousness and visualize a better future. The important thing to understand is that, although life may throw chaos your way, within the chaos you have a multitude of choices. Creating an intention is a way of setting aside your past stories to create a new one. It's a way of choosing how to put yourself out into the world. It's a way of connecting your best self with the opportunities before you.

   Creating intention is another way of declaring your purpose. I always ask clients to be specific: to not only declare a purpose, but also decide what steps to take to dedicate themselves to that purpose.

3. **Visualize Your New Story**: Visualizing is not just a magic trick. Research has shown that projecting sensory images in the mind that depict the results we wish to create has a real effect on psychological functioning. These mental pictures create measurable improvement in the results we achieve. Visualization opens the door to realizing our intentions.

   Much as you plan what to say before making a presentation, visualization is a way of planning your performance. Research by V. W. Donaldson in 2000 indicates that imagery may facilitate change in someone's psychological state by building confidence, promoting motivation, and reducing performance anxiety.[20] Visualization allows the brain to create an experience (data) you can later access when facing a similar real-life situation. The human body does not distinguish between an event that is experienced and one that is vividly imagined.

When we imagine something, neurological patterns emerge in response to the sensory images our minds create. That, in turn, leads to responses in our nerves and muscles. If we repeat a sequence of images, we strengthen that neural pathway. The result is that the responses we picture ourselves having in an imagined situation have a higher probability of occurring in an actual situation.

Amy was an administrator at a university who was working hard to advance into the position of public relations director. During a coaching session with Amy, I asked her to visualize the future she wanted. The idea was to create a story of how her future would look, sound, smell, taste, and feel. In her new story, she imagined the perceptions the other staff would have about her as she evolved from her support role to step out in front of people as a highly visible community leader.

After visualizing her future, Amy began to experience uncanny coincidences. In one instance, she received a call from a university alumnus. During the call, she recognized that the information this person was sharing represented a significant fundraising and public relations opportunity for the university foundation. She met with the foundation's executive director, told him about the alumnus inquiry, and shared her ideas about the opportunity. He asked her to take the lead in acting on the idea to create a fundraiser. This became a perfect opportunity to demonstrate her PR skills. She successfully worked with alumni to create the fundraiser, which is now an annual event.

What Amy experienced was synchronicity: the recognition of events transpiring in a way that suggested a connection, even though there was no clear cause-and-effect relationship between them. Carl Jung described this in his 1952 paper, "Synchronicity: An Acausal Connecting Principle," in which he asserted the importance of paying attention to coincidences and allowing ourselves to see meaning in the universe and our place in it.

I don't believe what Amy experienced was mere chance. By visualizing her story, she created an intention. This changed her awareness of what was already there and informed her behavior. She began to see opportunities she had not previously noticed.

In subsequent coaching sessions, Amy worked on gaining a greater understanding of her intentions, clearing out resistance to her goals, and moving from insight to action. She sought to increase her awareness of opportunities. When she noticed synchronicity, she acted on it as a manifestation of her subconscious desire to create a new future.

When you visualize the future you want, you prime your brain to recognize opportunities, illuminating a pathway through the chaos to your goals.

4. **Affirm Yourself and Continue the Process**: It's important to remind yourself of your visualized purpose and to measure your progress against the images you've created. Acknowledge each time you take action on synchronous opportunities. Also acknowledge each time you fail to do so, but instead of berating yourself for that, congratulate yourself for recognizing the path, and then recommit to staying on it. This way you'll know when you're on or off course.

    Moving in alignment with your purpose requires you to stay awake to what is happening both within and outside yourself, so that you can consciously make choices to move toward the new story you wish to create. As you move forward, seek to maintain detachment. If you catch yourself fretting or criticizing yourself when you recognize you're off course, acknowledge it and let it go. Accept every reminder of where you are in the process as a step forward. Congratulate yourself.

These new ways of resetting your story might not ring true at first. That's okay. You're relearning how to be in the world. Improving a new skill takes time.

Self-awareness is not a one-time discovery but something you must experience anew over and over. Sometimes it will elude you and you'll have to recapture it. Here is how you'll stay on the path to becoming a more aware leader: by knowing your thoughts, what they're focused on, and how they're affecting you in the world. If you're not attentive about keeping an objective eye on your thoughts and bringing them back to the present, you will miss the moment.

In any given moment, you might experience subtle signs of trouble or opportunity. You might become aware of the lessons a failure has to teach, or you might feel the fulfillment that comes with success. If you're not fully awake to those moments, you won't have all the information that can help you move forward, and you won't be able to lead.

More importantly, if you miss those moments, you will miss your life.

Get to Know Your Many Selves

Self-awareness is a practice that must be cultivated. One thing I've found helpful in getting to know myself is to recognize that I have many selves and to begin making distinctions between them. For the purpose of self-awareness, I suggest you consider four distinct selves that we all have: the thinking self, emotional self, functioning (physical) self, and the observing self, all of which Jon Kabat-Zinn addresses in his book, *Full Catastrophe Living*:

THE FOUR SELVES

1. **The Thinking Self:** This is the part of you that prattles away. It never shuts up. It always has something to say. It's probably babbling right now as you read this book. I would be surprised if it weren't. Don't be embarrassed. We all do it. At times, the thinking self does process useful information and make creative connections, so long as we keep it in check. One way to do that

is to remain aware of what the thinking self is saying. That gives us the opportunity to choose what we do with the information. It would be imprudent to act on every thought in our heads, but unless we're aware of what those thoughts are we run the risk of doing just that. On the journey to self-awareness, it never hurts to ask: *What is my thinking self saying to me now?*

2. **The Emotional Self:** This is the self that feels and deals with emotions. The emotional self also experiences your varying levels of self-esteem. What you choose to give your attention affects your emotions. So when people say they cannot choose how to feel, that's not completely true. Yes, sometimes emotions come up unbidden, but they come up based on where our focus is. If we want to move on to a new emotion, we can choose to do so by choosing a new arena to focus our attention.

   Selected attention regulates the amygdala, the part of the brain that processes raw emotions and reacts with primitive fight or flight responses. That's why it's important to develop a strong understanding of your emotional self, and how the things you give your attention can trigger different emotions. When you're more aware of the situations, people, and thoughts that trigger you, you increase your ability to make choices. You can choose how to spend your attention so that you can regulate your emotions. Then when emotions do come up, you can better choose how to respond.

   Leadership is largely about the power to choose. The more choices you give yourself to deal with emotions, the more effective you'll be at making rational choices, even in the heat of personal conflict, deadline pressure, or financial challenges.

3. **The Functioning (Physical) Self:** The functioning self is perhaps the most obvious, but that does not mean it is insignificant. Without it, none of the other selves would work. The functioning self comprises our health and wellbeing, how we feel physically from moment to moment, and our physical self-concept. People who are physically active and who have a positive physical self-concept—seeing themselves as attractive, strong, energetic, graceful, healthy, and capable—score higher

for psychological wellbeing, according to a 2011 study from university researchers in Spain.[21]

In that psychological study, researchers sampled 293 men and women, aged 18 to 70. They discovered that self-motivation significantly affects physical self-concept, and that a more positive physical self-concept is a significant contributor to greater satisfaction with life. The results led them to conclude that people who perform physical exercise regularly, and who make having fun an important part of their lives, tend to have better physical self-perception and, consequently, greater psychological wellbeing.

It's a timeless truth: a healthy body contributes to a healthy mind, and vice-versa.

4. **The Observing Self:** I talk about this self the most, but that's not because it's the only self you need to know. Rather, this is the self that is key to developing a deeper awareness of all the selves. What's more, it's also the self that's aware of your awareness itself. Where the other selves often overlap, the observing self tends to stand alone, apart from the thinking, emotional, and functioning selves. This is an important distinction, because the observing self notices the other selves without judgment. It's the part of your mind that can be aware of whatever you're thinking, feeling, or doing at any moment.

You cannot develop self-awareness without developing your observing self. Observing requires experiencing without judging or classifying the experience. To develop your observing self, you need to pay attention to what is happening both externally and internally.

Let's say you're giving a presentation and you experience racing thoughts, jumbled emotions, and sensations like sweating, a pounding heart, or an urge to pee. At a moment like that, you may be tempted to give up on your observing self. Don't. That's when it's most important. The observing self is the one who can take note of all those unsettling feelings and quiet them down. It can take you from feeling overwhelmed or distracted back to the present, by reminding you that underneath all that mental and physical busy-ness is the core of you, who can accept all of it and just be here now.

When you reach that moment, you're back in the driver's seat and can choose which direction you want to take the rest of the selves. It might feel like you're driving a clown car full of crazies, but don't let that scare you. When the observing self is driving, the others have little choice but to go wherever he or she points the car.

Build a Mindful Mind

Some people fear that self-awareness will require them to spend hours sitting in meditation. Although I do find meditation a highly useful practice for leaders, it is not a requirement. Another way to achieve the most important results associated with meditation is to simply practice mindfulness. When your observing self is in charge, that's exactly what you're doing: being mindful.

Being mindful of your naturally arising thoughts, feelings, and sensations will help you overcome the grip of thoughts, feelings, and sensations that don't serve you. By impartially observing your thoughts, feelings, and sensations as they come and go, you internalize the truth we all know but often forget: that they do indeed come and go. Recognizing the impermanence of our mental, emotional, and physical states reduces the feeling that we're at their mercy. Noticing what goes on in your mind without reacting to it douses automatic avoidance and fear responses. The goal is to allow yourself to experience whatever is happening in the moment.

What is mindfulness? In short, it means developing the ability to be fully present in the moment. It is about slowing down and seeking opportunities to open your mind to all possibilities. Because my clients are busy executives, it is all the more important for them to engage in mindfulness so they stay energetic and present, attuned to the matters of the moment. Yet, also because they're busy, they cannot always spend a lot of time trying to achieve that mindful state. They need to find fast, easy ways to do it.

Be aware of your thoughts so that you don't get caught up in them. Especially don't confuse your thoughts with reality.

Whatever you do to keep yourself mindful, it must fit your lifestyle, priorities, and values, or you won't be able to make it a habit, and making mindfulness a habit is critical if you want true ongoing self-awareness. Some activities I recommend include: jogging, walking, reflecting, praying, journaling, listening to music, and yes...meditation.

In the July 2013 issue of *Wired* magazine, Noah Shachtman's article, "Enlightenment Engineers," says of the movers and shakers of Silicon Valley that they no longer use coffee to stay alert. Instead, "quiet contemplation is seen as the new caffeine, the type of fuel that allegedly unlocks productivity and creative bursts." Shachtman says that numerous studies have shown meditation to improve memory and the ability to respond to changing situations, manage time, focus, plan, and organize. Boston University researchers have demonstrated that, after as little as three and a half hours of meditation training, subjects reacted less to emotionally charged images.[22]

That does not mean you need to spend three hours meditating to see results. By investing just a few minutes of being mindful periodically throughout the day, you can ultimately *save* much more than those few minutes in time and effort, because this practice will improve your productivity and creativity.

If you still think you're too busy to be mindful, or if sitting still and staring inward just isn't for you, here is one alternative I find helpful that you can do in as little as one minute:

MINDFUL MOMENT #2
DEEP BREATHING

Objective: Deep breathing is an easy, effective way to calm yourself when you're stressed. It has the power to short-circuit the mental chatter that keeps you worrying about the future or stewing over the past, instead returning your mind to the present. Just two minutes of deep breathing can help you feel more present in the moment and more relaxed throughout the day.

Instructions:

1. Sit up straight. Keep your backbone upright and shoulders pulled back.
2. Inhale slowly and deeply. Think about how pure, fresh, and cleansing this new air is for your body.
3. Focus on how your lungs feel as they expand with air. Pay attention to how your diaphragm moves to make room for more air in your lungs.
4. Exhale slowly. Release the air from your lungs until they are completely empty. Feel your lungs contract as you expel the old air from your body.
5. Visualize your stress being released as you exhale. See all of your tension being released from your body and dissipating into the air.
6. Repeat these steps multiple times. As you do, notice how your body relaxes and you start to feel more present.
7. Practice deep breathing regularly. Each time you start feeling stressed about your day, use this exercise to calm down. With practice, it will take less and less time.

Let's take a look at a few simple and sometimes unexpected ways my clients, friends, and I tailor mindful moments to fit our unique lifestyles:

A friend of mine starts every day with meditation, sitting silently in a perfect lotus position for an hour every morning. That's how he stays in tune with who he is. It's impressive. When I started mindfulness practices, I could only meditate for about five minutes at a crack, and I could barely cross my legs much less manage lotus. But although I admire my friend, I don't worry that I'm missing something because I can't do what he does. I start my day by asking myself to enter conscious awareness. That's all I need to get into the mindset of mindfulness.

If you simply start the day by sitting or standing still for five minutes and bringing yourself into the present moment, that's mindfulness. You can even do this in the shower. Once you're fully present, you can make mental notes: "I've got that meeting at three... I've got that conflict with so-and-so to address... I have that email to write." It's a straightforward technique that you can use to prepare for your day with a greater level of awareness.

Once you get into that habit, you can add mindful moments throughout the day: bits of time when you pause what you're doing, check in with yourself, and ask yourself simple questions, such as, "How's the day going so far?" or engage in simple visualizations, such as, "What's next?"

Many of my clients find it helpful to ask their observing self to reflect on whatever experience they've just completed. Two simple questions can provide you closure on what just passed while making space for what's next: 1) *At that last meeting, what was I doing when I was at my best?* 2) *Is there something I can do next time to be even more effective?* The second question is not meant to be negative, but simply to provide you with self-feedback. We all can be more effective, and reflection is a good way to consider how.

I often refer my clients to an evergreen article in the *Harvard Business Review*, called "Manage Your Energy, Not Your Time." The article points out how subjective our experience of time really is. We all have the same amount of time, yet we all talk about it so differently. That article has reinforced for me the idea that, rather than trying to wedge more time into the day, it's more useful to consciously create positive energy moments throughout the day.[23]

If you want to inject some positive energy into your day, I suggest focusing on four energy areas: 1) emotional, 2) physical, 3) spiritual, and 4) mental.

Negative things happen to all of us every day, and in the life of an executive they can pile up fast. Let's go back to Amy, the university PR director, who is very talented but tends to get tense throughout the day because one of her default settings is perfectionism. Her constant tension was becoming an energy drain and she needed a way to recharge.

So I asked her, "What are some things you could do to change the energy for you?"

"I can take a ten-minute walk," she said. "Right outside my office is a pretty path into the woods."

Perfect! It cost no money and little time, but those ten minutes in nature made a huge difference in keeping her calm, energized, and focused throughout the rest of her day.

What works for Amy won't work for everyone. Every leader works in different circumstances and has different values and needs. Sam, who is the head of sales at his company, came up with what may be the most creative personal solution to the problem of "I need to get mindful, but I don't have time." What stresses Sam out is that he never went to college and he fears that people will find out his secret. He needed a strong hook to take him out of that emotional trap and return him to the moment.

We were sitting in his office when I asked him, "What things do you have in your life that bring you joy?"

His answer was immediate: "Music." He explained that he plays guitar and listens to an eclectic variety of music. His face lit up as he talked about his favorite artist.

I looked around his office and immediately saw his dilemma. "Steve, I've got to ask you a question. If you love music and it's one of the few things that relax you, why is there no music in this room at all? I don't see headphones, speakers, a stereo, an iPod. Nothing."

He looked around as if seeing his office for the first time. He suggested that maybe he had thought of anything that smacked of entertainment as a distraction.

I suggested that Steve's love of music was an opportunity to bring him back into the moment in almost no time, anytime he needed a refresher. Most songs are just three or four minutes. "I wonder what would happen if just two or three times during the day, you set aside three minutes and forty-two seconds to listen to the music that you love."

He smiled as if I had given him permission to play hooky. Quite the opposite: this was not going to distract him. It was bound to bring him back into his body so he could relax and focus.

The next time I visited him, he had a heck of a stereo system in his office, plus some high-end headphones that he had researched to death and couldn't wait to tell me about. Now whenever Sam is stressed and feels himself getting sucked into the chatter in his head, he spends a few minutes listening to music and creates a positive energy moment for himself. That snaps him back into the moment, and he's ready for the next meeting. Not only that, he brings that energy into the meeting with him, which has a positive impact on his team and those he leads.

Sam still has the voice in his head that worries somebody might find out he doesn't have the education most people in his position have. But when the music is turned up in his headphones, that other voice gets turned down low and stays that way for hours. It helps him disengage from the negative story he has been telling himself for years.

As you get to know yourself, you'll discover your own ways to inject positive energy into your day and increase your mindfulness. This is a journey to yourself, and ultimately only you can choose the best way to get there, including all the little moments along the way.

A WORD TO THE AWARE LEADER:

May my mind come alive today
To the invisible geography
That invites me to new frontiers,
To break the dead shell of yesterdays,
To risk being disturbed and changed.
May I have the courage today
To live the life that I would love,
To postpone my dream no longer
But do at last what I came here for
And waste my heart on fear no more.

— John O'Donahue,
To Bless the Space Between Us: A Book of Blessings

FIVE

OFF THE TRACKS

The Big Engine That Couldn't

When a train runs off the tracks, we call that a derailment. We all face moments when something unexpected throws us for such a loop that we too run "off the tracks." The worst of these moments can severely impact, even ruin, our lives and careers, as well as the lives and careers of others. Managers once lauded as rising stars may stop rising, get fired, find themselves at the center of scandals that make it difficult to ever get hired again, or even land in prison. Executives who derail typically take others down with them, costing their companies big money and costing their employees jobs or opportunities.

Executive derailment is a constant problem in today's business world. We regularly hear that this or that business has crumbled, and one commonly cited factor is an executive who went off the rails.

Although external pressures such as institutional change, increased competition, or financial pressure contribute to executive derailment, a leader who is likely to jump the tracks usually exhibits derailing behaviors from the start. In any case, stress is not a good excuse. Executives are chosen to deal with change, competition, and financial challenges, so the very nature of their job demands an ability to manage stress. Derailment indicates a lack of fit between an individual and the evolving demands of the job. Stress simply amplifies a leader's usual characteristics.

Perhaps one of the harshest ironies of the executive track is that many of the qualities that help people rise to the top don't work as well at keeping them there. What leaders need is self-awareness of the double-edged sword their personal qualities may represent.

There are four key dynamics that lead to derailment:

1. **An Early Strength Becomes a Weakness:** The same skills and characteristics that enable you to excel early in your career can become liabilities if you reach a managerial position and don't develop new skills. For example, a diligent, conscientious, task-focused contributor accustomed to working independently to achieve results might find it hard to work with teams or subordinates.

2. **A Flaw That Didn't Matter Before, Eventually Does:** We all have qualities that can show up as shortcomings. Among managers, some shortcomings likely to be cited by colleagues and employees are: narcissism, passive-aggression, and skepticism. Most executives have two or three flaws, which might not surface right away. Some leaders initially compensate for flaws with other strengths, but that becomes less effective as they move to higher levels of responsibility. For example, a manager might be identified as having potential because he's sharp, energetic, and results-oriented, even though he's also arrogant, short-fused, and abrasive. He might move to a senior position, only to find that his lack of interpersonal skills limits his effectiveness in managing teams or motivating employees.

3. **A Hidden Flaw Surfaces Under Extreme or Unexpected Challenges:** A manager might face unexpected challenges brought on by changes in an organization. Such changes can come from any direction: an economic downturn, new regulations, or maybe an internal crisis in the organization. Under pressure they've never experienced before, leaders sometimes react in ways that never came up before. For example, a

manager might freeze when faced with the reality that every choice available is going to hurt somebody.

4. **A Previously Effective Leader Becomes a Victim of Their Own Success:** Managers who have enjoyed early success sometimes develop an unrealistic sense of superiority and infallibility, which can affect their judgment and their receptivity to alternative ideas. Sometimes this type of manager will resort to tried-and-true but ineffective solutions rather than risk experimenting with new strategies that might fail. As a result, they fail to adapt to the evolving demands of new situations.

At one time or another, we can all become susceptible to derailing behaviors. Most of these behaviors arise from our default settings, which refer to our distorted beliefs about ourselves, how others will treat us, and the best means to achieve our goals. When we were children, we established our default settings to help us develop strategies to deal with anxiety and to make sense of our relationships, primarily with our parents. As I conveyed in Chapter Three, default settings are resistant to change. So how do we keep them from derailing us? We do that through increased self-awareness. We explore, discover, and accept what our default settings are. Then we come up with new choices about how to deal with them.

Let's say you tend to react to change by making decisions based on fear. In that case, maybe you need to learn to recognize the internal indicators that signal you're afraid, and then hold off on making decisions at those moments. Or maybe you need to give yourself more choices within the context of fear. Afraid to pursue a new project because it might pose too big a financial risk? Then maybe you give yourself other fears to compare and contrast with that one, such as the financial risk entailed in a business remaining stagnant and failing to respond to a changing market. Or maybe you need to make the change in increments, so you can face your fears in small doses over time.

Here's one more option: Maybe you need to allow yourself to feel fear, but make the choice you would make if fear were not a factor. This can give you a chance to experience courage, which is not the absence of fear but rather the willingness to act in spite of it.

Do you see how all the above options do not change your default settings, but simply allow you to express them differently so that they don't derail you?

How Jim's Childhood Derailed Him

For several years, I have provided leadership assessments and executive coaching for a nonprofit organization that equips high-potential minorities to reach their potential. Jim was one of those in this group who scored disproportionately low on the "good attachment" scale. Good attachment measures the strength of relationships created in childhood. Low scores often indicate that the test subject experienced an especially difficult childhood, such as growing up with abusive, demanding, or absent parents. Many of these leaders overcame huge obstacles to get where they are. Unfortunately, sometimes the compensating behaviors they developed, such as an inability to trust, don't serve them well in the higher ranks.

Jim grew up in his city's urban projects. He had a strong relationship with his mother, but his father was absent. His attachment issues had more to do with the neighborhood where he lived. Whenever he left his apartment to go to school, he was all too aware he was leaving the safe, predictable haven he and his brother shared with their loving mother, only to enter violent, unpredictable streets. His mother warned him to always be on the lookout for danger. "Trust no one," she told him. She instilled in him that education was his ticket out. Thanks to his mother's training in vigilance, he and his brother survived, excelled in school, escaped the projects for college, and went on to build great careers.

Jim became a successful trader for a global bank. He navigated his way through his career much as he had made it through school: being a loner, watching over his shoulder, and not calling attention to himself. His teachers would likely have described him as someone who keeps his nose to the grindstone.

At the bank, Jim's intellect, hard work, and results were recognized and rewarded. He was promoted to an executive director position, managing a team of traders. With that, he knew he could no longer work alone but would be called upon to become a team player. The problem was that his ability to play alone was what had helped him escape his neighborhood, where "team" meant "gang." Still, he was determined to make a go of it because it was another chance to create distance from his tough childhood, support his mother, and grow into a brighter future.

Jim continued to do well at those things he knew how to do well: moved carefully, behaved conscientiously, set high standards, and watched out for everything. Those represented the useful aspects of his default settings. But those defaults hid derailing behaviors: he remained hypervigilant, he acted suspicious of the actions and intentions of others, he micromanaged, and he became controlling. One of his controlling behaviors was an inability to delegate authority. By failing to do that, he created extra pressure for himself and deprived others of the opportunity to learn. Although he had started with the intention of learning to work with a team, when that proved difficult he kept to himself, convincing himself he worked better alone.

Both Jim's performance and his team's performance suffered. His team experienced him as picky, critical, and stubborn. He tried to make up for the team's low performance and discontent by taking on yet more of the workload. In some ways, he felt as if he were back in the projects, watching over his shoulder and struggling to survive. These behaviors did not go unnoticed. His supervisor intervened. He still believed in Jim's potential, but concluded he was not ready to take things to the next level. He offered Jim a chance to go back to his old job.

What derailed Jim? During his early life his skepticism and vigilance were rewarded with survival. His self-reliance was rewarded with eluding gang life and succeeding in school. Throughout his early life he saw evidence that few people were doing good work besides him, so he developed the belief that if he wanted things done right he should do them himself. He felt validated in his mode of operating when he was hired by a bank, recognized for his work, and promoted. Unfortunately for Jim, he did not realize that the very attributes that initially helped him survive and succeed, would ultimately lead to his failure further up the hierarchy.

I watched Jim do the hard work to develop self-awareness of his skepticism, vigilance, and tendency to isolate. He told me, "I have to be aware of it at times because I'll get into a situation where I think there's some risk for me. Now it's career risk, but it reminds me of those old risks that were dangerous." These days he is more aware when he perceives a threat, and he is able to pause before he reacts to consider whether the threat is real or smaller than it seems. When his skepticism surfaces, he now has choices about how to deal with it.

Jim will never completely lose his skepticism, and that's a good thing. Healthy skepticism can serve us all in some situations, such as negotiations, where we need to be aware of competing agendas.

In fact, lack of skepticism can be a problem too. I sometimes work with clients who score low on skepticism. Their default setting may be naiveté, which can lead to the derailing behavior of trusting everyone too much. Part of your job as an aware leader is to ascertain whether you have the right sort of performers on your team, and that requires some skepticism. If not, you could find that you have someone on your team who promises to deliver something they can't. However, once you form a team, it's time to dial down the skepticism and dial up the trust, empowering and inspiring others to perform.

We all must find a way to ride the fine line, that place of balance where we don't blindly follow our best qualities or run away from our worst qualities, but instead figure out when and how each of our qualities has the power to serve us or fail us.

If you remember one thing about Jim's derailing behaviors, let it be this: they were for the most part involuntary. That is, he was not at conscious choice when he engaged in them. What Jim needed was not to change, but to become self-aware.

"I'm afraid that sometimes
you'll play lonely games too.
Games you can't win
'cause you'll play against you." — Dr. Seuss

Jim has since been promoted to a midlevel executive position and is now in his company's high-potential development program. He did something the best leaders do: instead of seeing the return to his old job as a defeat, he used it as a catalyst to learn more about himself, receive executive coaching, and tone down the effects of his skepticism. He has redirected his survival instincts, developing new survival skills for a new environment. Letting go and trusting is still a challenge, but he knows how to connect the dots between his early survival story and the way that it enters his life as a leader. That gives him new choices about how to respond.

The Biggest Derailer

The derailing behavior that trips most people up, by far, is *diligence*, otherwise known as perfectionism. It sounds positive. In fact, some people actually *like* listing it as their worst flaw because it allows them to boast without seeming to. But diligence can be a real problem when set too high, leading to such behaviors as micromanaging, indecisiveness, and an inability to meet deadlines. Diligence is the behavior that's most resistant to change. Fortunately, this book is not about *changing* who you are, but about becoming *aware* of who you are.

Diligence typically comes from growing up in an exacting family, where if you made the smallest mistake there was hell to pay. Diligent children learn to prevent punishment by trying to do everything perfectly, as well as trying to control everything around them.

I've coached a CEO in the manufacturing industry who scores high on diligence. When Cal was growing up, his father traveled a lot for work and was rarely home. When he was home, he was exacting about the behavior he expected. Cal grew up trying desperately to please this man, because he had so few opportunities to do so, and perhaps in the hope that it might keep his father home. The lack of loving attention also motivated his empathy and altruism, or he might have become a tyrant.

Still, in adulthood, Cal's diligence became a potential derailer for him as a leader because he felt anxious unless he had his hands in every detail of his operation. He was working seven days a week trying to stay on top of it all, and he was so smart he got away with that most of the way up the ladder. But a CEO cannot be involved in every aspect of operations. Cal had to let go of some of it. He had to learn to delegate, and to prioritize what to perfect and what to leave at "good enough."

Awareness of his perfectionism was key. That allowed Cal to choose how to apply his admirable desire to do well. That desire will never go away, but today it serves him better.

Identifying Your Potential Derailers

Because we live in a busy world, we all live a good portion of our lives autonomically. Learning to accomplish many tasks without thinking about them—breathing, making coffee, scheduling appointments, reading up on industry trends—frees our minds for solving problems, creating ideas, and producing new products and services. However, our goal as leaders should be to increase our options for engaging in conscious actions that we can choose.

Derailment is almost always involuntary. Why would anyone crash their company, team, or career on purpose? Executive derailment is always a nasty surprise, to both the individual and the organization. It is rarely caused by a lack of knowledge, experience, or skills, but instead is typically caused by the leader's lack of awareness of their own behavior, and of the styles and preferences that lead to that behavior.

Avoiding derailment does not require changing your default settings. Rather, it requires getting to know yourself and your derailers so they don't take you by surprise. Although staying on top of that is optimally a lifelong effort, one way to begin is by working with an executive coach, consultant, or leadership training professional to assess your behaviors, styles, and preferences. If you do, you'll want to start with professional assessment tools to identify the areas you and your coach need to focus on to develop your self-awareness and potential areas for growth.

Let's take a look at a couple of assessment tools with good track records:

Benchmarks® is a 360-degree manager assessment created by the Center For Creative Leadership, which has been used by more than 16,000 organizations and 200,000 leaders. It identifies five personal qualities that have high potential to derail leaders.

Benchmarks'® Five Potential Career Derailers:

1. "Problems with interpersonal relationships" — This refers to managers who isolate themselves, and/or act authoritarian, aloof, arrogant, and insensitive.
2. "Difficulty leading a team" — This refers to managers who fail to staff effectively, cannot build or lead a team, or are unable to handle conflict.
3. "Difficulty changing or adapting" — This refers to managers who are unable to adapt to bosses or colleagues with different managerial or interpersonal styles, and who are unable to learn, develop, and think strategically.
4. "Failure to meet business objectives" — This refers to managers who overreach in their ambitions or lack follow-through.
5. "Too narrow functional orientation" — This refers to managers who are unable to manage new situations and people outside of their current functions.

The Hogan Development Survey (HDS) is another leading psychometric assessment tool. It has been used to assess more than two million working adults with more than 450 different jobs. HDS identifies eleven derailing tendencies: personal characteristics and behaviors that can lead to derailment. Executives who scale high on those eleven tendencies often exhibit positive versions of those behaviors that are prone to become negative under stress.

11 HDS DERAILERS THAT MOVE FROM POSITIVE TO NEGATIVE UNDER STRESS:		
Derailer	Manager changes from being:	To seeming:
1) Excitable	Intense & energetic	Moody and overreacting
2) Skeptical	Perceptive & shrewd	Cynical & mistrustful
3) Cautious	Careful & thorough	Reluctant to take risks
4) Reserved	Independent & businesslike	Stoic & disconnected
5) Leisurely	Cooperative & agreeable	Covertly resistant & insincere
6) Bold	Confident & assertive	Stubborn, arrogant, & smug
7) Mischievous	Charming & jocular	Irreverent & untrustworthy
8) Colorful	Outgoing & animated	Showboating & overwhelming
9) Imaginative	Innovative & creative	Off-the-wall & unrealistic
10) Diligent	Detail oriented & hardworking	Perfectionistic & demanding
11) Dutiful	Supportive & loyal	Ingratiating & deferential

I've assessed thousands of executives using the HDS, and have found that most score high on one or more of the eleven scales. Those high scores represent a double-edged sword: the strongest leadership qualities are typically also the greatest potential derailers. Without these strengths, leaders could not have climbed the heights of their chosen fields in the first place.

As leaders, we cannot assume that whatever got us this far will take us the rest of the way. It behooves us to know which strengths have the potential to turn on us under stress. The higher we rise in an organization, the more likely that triggers for stress will increase. We need to plan for situations in which letting our inner selves rise to the surface might not serve us. If your derailers haven't reared their ugly heads yet, don't let that make you complacent. They are waiting within all of us, Jack-in-the-Boxes waiting to pop up at inconvenient times.

I recommend four steps to identify and stay on top of your potential derailing behaviors:

STAY ON TOP OF YOUR DERAILERS

1. Assess: Take a leadership assessment under the guidance of certified professionals who can help you understand the results.
2. Seek feedback: Solicit 360-feedback from everyone who works with you, from employees to team members to those you report to. Review past feedback.
3. Observe: Develop a practice of calling on your observing self to objectively track your internal life and external behavior. Look for patterns. Without judgment, check in with yourself on which behaviors yield results and which don't. Find compassion for yourself when you engage in habitual behaviors, create opportunities to disengage from those behaviors, and consider all the choices at your disposal.
4. Know your stress triggers and indicators: Stay aware of your body's reactions to perceived threats. Be mindful of your thoughts and emotions, staying on the lookout for fear, uncertainty, or damaging self-talk. Stay aware of stress symptoms such as headaches, insomnia, or rumination. Be mindful of changes, conflicts, or unpredictable events that come up.

When you identify and understand the sources of your stress, you take the first step in learning to better manage it. Manage it, not eliminate it. Stress is a fact of life.

Observation Can Prevent Derailment

Many of our default settings relate to the way our brains have evolved, a process over which we have no control. The human brain has had about 450 million years to develop its most primitive functions, only about 10 million years to develop its more rational functions, and, some researchers estimate, only around 100,000 years to develop the final cell layers that determine our brain as uniquely human. We are less in control than we think.

Luckily, we have the relatively new ability to observe our behavior and make choices based on our observations. When it comes to using this new "observer" part of the brain, we're like toddlers just learning to walk. Go easy on yourself. You might fall down a few times. That's a normal part of learning. As you train your observing self to recognize when you need to pause and re-center rather than react, that strengthens your ability to choose your behavior.

Four Types of Observation Can Increase Your Choices:

1. Internal: what and how you think in different life situations, the stories you carry
2. Interpersonal: how you respond to others and to conflicts involving other individuals
3. Intrapersonal: how you respond to others and to conflicts involving groups
4. Organizational: how you respond to others or to conflicts, problems, or situations in the context of an organization, or what choices you make at an organizational level Default Settings and Derailment

If you don't practice self-awareness, you empower your default settings to take you unaware and derail you. Based on information from the Hogan Development Survey Manual, we can extrapolate that some childhood experiences may be more likely to lead to derailing behaviors in adult life. To aid your quest to gain awareness and avoid derailment, see if any of the potential derailers listed below, or the childhood dynamics associated with them, resonate with you.[24] If so, they might be worth further investigation so you can create strategies to address situations and thought patterns that threaten to derail you.

Potential Derailers — Adapted from the Hogan Development Survey Manual

Excitability: Do you tend to be moody and hard to please? Do you have a tendency to erupt? Do you long for acceptance but expect rejection? It's likely you grew up in an unpredictable and emotionally volatile family in which behaviors that were praised one day might be punished the next. In such a family, the adults often negate the child's feelings and opinions, making it difficult for the child to develop a cohesive identity.

Skepticism: Do you typically feel on high alert, have difficulty trusting others, and get offended easily? This may be because you grew up in an environment that was degrading, controlling, or dishonest. As a child you would have survived your hostile environment by becoming unusually self-sufficient, believing you were the only person you could count on.

Caution: Do you have trouble asserting yourself? Are you often defensive? Do you fear mistakes, criticism, and embarrassment? This one is pretty straightforward: you likely grew up in a family that was critical, offering inconsistent criteria for approval and affection.

Reserve: Do you have a hard time being open or remembering to show concern for the feelings of others? Do other people sometimes find you aloof or insensitive? If so, your early experiences were likely marked by social isolation and by inadequate nurturing from parents or caregivers. Adults may have insisted you be self-sufficient from a very young age.

Leisurely Attitude: Do you often offer surface cooperation while privately feeling irritable about shouldering more than your share? Do you say you'll do something you don't want to do, but find ways not to cooperate? As a child, perhaps you enjoyed attention that was withdrawn abruptly and replaced by demands for high performance. The adults in your life likely expected you to always do as told, no questions asked, and never to express frustration.

Boldness: Are you more self-confident than most, always certain you're competent for every task, even those you've never done? Are you convinced you're special in a way few understand? This often results when parents consistently treat a son or daughter like a "golden child," giving continuous positive feedback and failing to provide boundaries. A child who grows up in such an environment does not learn the value of dealing with failure.

Mischievous Behavior: Are you a socially smooth person who seeks to dominate others to avoid being dominated? Do you act carefree even when the world seems to be falling apart around you? Are you an excitement seeker who feels a rush from taking risks? Such people were often raised in families that provided inconsistent nurturing and control. In such a family, you would have learned that only the strong and the cunning survive.

Colorful Personality: Are you a drama queen, or king, who thrives on being the center of attention? Do you tend to experience attention as a sign of achievement? Then you may come from a background in which attention and affirmation were based more on your charm, appearance, or capacity to entertain, and less on your competence, persistence, or achievement.

Imagination: Imagination can be positive, but ask yourself whether you ever embrace going beyond the imaginative to the odd and eccentric. Do you often emphasize creativity at the expense of practicality? Adults who let imagination run away with them usually had early experiences that minimized adherence to social convention in favor of creative expression.

Diligence: Are you compulsively meticulous and conscientious to the point of perfectionism? Do you have trouble seeing beyond just two options in any endeavor: perfection or failure? That suggests you grew up in an environment where adults overvalued high performance and excessively criticized failed efforts.

Duty: Are you a people-pleaser, especially with those in authority? Do you find it easier to be ingratiating than take action on your own? Such people typically grew up with parents so nurturing they failed to pull back and allow a child to develop independence and experience self-efficacy. Such children don't experience competence, but rely on others to tell them what to do.

Once you know which of the above derailers are the ones you need to keep an eye out for, here are a few ways you can use that knowledge to empower yourself:

- **Naming** – Naming your derailing behaviors, instead of entertaining vague notions that you "have issues," makes them real for you, giving you something specific to work with. Naming a derailer clarifies your perception of it, empowering you to construct new perceptions. I suggest you don't just use the names listed above but instead come up with your own simple names that are specific to you and your experience of the derailer. For example, your derailer might feel more like "avoidance" than "caution." Or "control" might strike you as a more apt term for your behavior than "diligence."
- **Accepting** – Accept your derailers. We all have them. Here's the paradox: change occurs when you first accept who you *are* rather than trying to become what you are *not*.
- **Developing Strategies** – Develop strategies to deal with challenging situations that might trigger derailing behavior. Give yourself options for alternative behaviors. Now that you have named your derailing responses, when you feel one coming on, its name is your new signal to put your strategy into effect. Strategies abound within your experiences, feedback from others, research, mentors, trial and error, and observations. A great place to start is to think back to similar situations you have successfully navigated in the past.
- **Anticipating** – Begin each day reflecting on who you are, how you want to show up, and what you want to accomplish. Anticipate both the opportunities and the landmines the day might present. Moving this information into your consciousness allows you to move beyond automatic responses to every stimulus, and to recognize those stimuli that require special attention. This gives you greater choice when challenges arise.

- **Pausing** – Mindfulness increases your chance of acting on the new strategies you've planned. We practice mindfulness when we do things like pausing in the midst of a busy day to take a breath, sit back, and look around, taking in sensory impressions of the space and people around us as if experiencing them for the first time. Pausing to experience the moment prepares us to be fully present when challenges arise.
- **Reflecting** – As you grow in self-awareness, you start the day by setting intentions. A natural bookend to that is to end the day with reflection. This allows you to build a sense of efficacy to deal with whatever tomorrow brings. Reflect on your day in a non-judgmental way, embracing both successes and failures as learning opportunities.

As you become more self-aware, things may seem to get worse before they get better. This is probably *not* because you're engaging in more derailing behavior, but because you're more aware of it. If, despite your efforts, derailing behavior emerges, don't fret. It happens to us all. The great news is that you *are* aware of it. With that awareness, you can develop strategies to mitigate the unwanted effects and do better tomorrow. That's what aware leaders do.

A WORD TO THE AWARE LEADER:

If your emotional abilities aren't in hand, if you don't have self-awareness, if you are not able to manage your distressing emotions, if you can't have empathy and have effective relationships, then no matter how smart you are, you are not going to get very far.

—Daniel Goleman

SIX

HARNESS YOUR EMOTIONS

Emotions Are Not the Enemy

In an effort to avoid derailing behavior, you might feel tempted to set aside your emotions. After all, if derailing behavior comes from default settings, and default settings come from childhood experiences, then allowing emotions to influence our choices must be a mistake, right? Wrong! It is not emotions that adversely influence our behavior, but *lack of awareness* about our emotions.

Emotions play a critical role in your life as a leader. The more aware you are of your emotions and what prompts them, the more choices you have.

In modern life, we're socialized to believe that emotion clouds judgment. Sure, expressing extreme emotions like unchecked rage or excessive exuberance can damage the social relationships we rely on. But if we don't demonstrate passion for what we do, and if we cannot inspire others to pursue their work with passion, we are not really leading.

87

It's a common misconception that it's unprofessional to bring our emotions to work because people might view us as weak. Yet how can we inspire others or support them in their endeavors if we never demonstrate sincere enthusiasm or empathy? We've been misled to think we must never bring our personal problems to work. Yet how can we build the friendships that will strengthen our network, if we don't allow ourselves to share confidences and show vulnerability to those with whom we want to build trust? As leaders, we sometimes fear that showing enthusiastic approval of our employees will undermine our authority, when in actuality our approval can foster a sense of loyalty, belonging, and motivation in our teams.

A leader's emotions play a central role in encouraging creativity, fostering new ideas, and fueling competitive energy. A leader who recognizes how to harness emotions can put them to work as part of the functional engine that makes an organization run at peak performance.

Why Phil Needed to Get Emotional

Phil was a brilliant geophysicist I coached at a high point in his career, a point when leaders often find support useful as they adjust to shifting roles. His organization had just asked him to lead his first team. When I assessed Phil, he scored high on the Hogan scale for Adjustment. That looked great on paper because it implied resilience, optimism, and composure, but it also hinted that at times Phil came across as overconfident and resistant to feedback.[3]14

Phil is a scientist who relies primarily on logic. For Phil, emotions don't always compute. This might sound like it would make for an efficient and well-reasoned decision process. However, it does not always serve him as a leader, because it also means he has a narrow range of affect—that is, he does not display much emotion. His inability to clearly demonstrate joy, love, anger, fear, or sadness makes it hard for him to connect with others, limiting his ability to motivate them to achievement or reassure them in a crisis. Phil's other good-news/bad-news challenge is that he's off-the-charts brilliant. On one hand, people trust his ideas. On the other hand, it can be difficult for him to communicate those ideas, especially when the "know-it-all" side of him emerges.

Phil once told me, "I'll get in these situations in which somebody is explaining something, and I've already moved on because I know the answer. I get impatient and upset that they're wasting my time. Why don't they get it?"

I knew it was important for him to get a handle on the emotional picture here, so I asked, "How do those people leave that conversation? Do you think they feel like they've been heard?"

He admitted they probably didn't. "I know I have to work on that."

That is key to his success: knowing he has to work on that. He scores in the top five percent of high-potential executives, and he can stay on that path if he remains aware of his emotional states and does his best to also recognize the emotions of his team.

If Phil's emotional life were music, he would come across like a children's song, playing just a few notes. On the other end of the spectrum are people who let their emotions run away with them, which is great when they're playing a symphony of exuberance, but not so great when panic or rage take over the show. The trick is to know what prompts your emotions, how emotions show up in your decisions, and the way your emotions push or pull others.

When you know what the effects of your emotions are at the extreme ends of the spectrum, you can find new ways to make them work for you instead of against you.

Phil learned to recognize his impatience and how it could lead him to be dismissive or irritable with others. He learned to curb that impatience and, rather than focusing on other people's inability to understand him, instead focus on opportunities to learn about how others think. He repurposed his inquiring mind to ask questions and listen to responses. This helped him understand where someone else might be stuck, and to realize when he missed information.

Phil still comes to quick conclusions and doesn't often change his mind. Nevertheless, people respond to his new style, feeling they are being heard and respected, and that he is connecting emotionally. Phil has discovered that understanding the way others think, especially his direct reports, makes him more effective at mentoring them and influencing their actions.

Mastering Emotional Intelligence

Emotions motivate us. In turn, we can channel our emotions to motivate others. Research has long demonstrated a correlation between emotional intelligence and success. In the 2009 book, *The Extraordinary Leader: Turning Good Managers into Great Leaders*, authors John Zenger and Joseph Folkman point out that when leaders come crashing down due to fatal flaws, "the fatal flaws are not intellectual deficiencies, but much more on the 'emotional intelligence' or interpersonal side of the equation. These flaws arise from emotional and behavioral dimensions and seldom from a dearth of knowledge or technical incompetence."25

People are the building blocks of every organization. People create, make, and sell an organization's products and services. People manage an organization's systems. All people are motivated by emotions. That is why true leadership calls for emotional mastery.

"Emotional intelligence is more rare than book smarts, but my experience says it is actually more important in the making of a leader—you just can't ignore it." — Jack Welch, Former CEO of General Electric

Many researchers have found that emotional intelligence, or EQ, is a greater predictor of success in life than cognitive intelligence quotient, or IQ. Psychologists Peter Salovey, now president of Yale, and John D. Mayer, of the University of New Hampshire, pioneered the concept of emotional intelligence in 1990, defining it as the capacity to understand emotional information and to reason using emotions.[26] They divided emotional intelligence into four areas:

FOUR BRANCHES OF EMOTIONAL INTELLIGENCE (SALOVEY AND MAYER):

1. The capacity to accurately perceive emotions
2. The capacity to use emotions to facilitate thinking
3. The capacity to understand emotional meanings
4. The capacity to manage emotions

If you agree with me that self-awareness is a key to effective leadership, and if emotional intelligence is a key predictor of success, then it makes sense for you as a leader to seek an intimate awareness of your emotions and how they impact you and others.

What are emotions? One way of looking at it is that they are interpretations that give meaning to the physical sensations in our bodies. Emotions affect our perceptions, decisions, and actions. Emotions serve as a guide in our communication with others.

Emotions are not our enemy. They are integral to the human experience. They only become problems when we either let them run us, or we judge them as wrong or inappropriate. When we let emotions run us, we are so busy flailing in their grip that we miss the messages they carry. When we judge our emotions, stuffing them down for fear of what they might make us do, they don't go away but instead hide under the surface, ticking time bombs waiting to explode.

What, then, is emotional mastery? Immature people treat emotions like trading stamps: collecting feelings and hording them until they become outdated to others but build in value for the collector. Sooner or later, the collector hauls out those feelings to trade them in for a psychological prize, usually at someone else's expense. Emotional mastery is the ability to process our emotions so that we receive their messages, and to use those messages to help us decide on appropriate action, avoiding the unconscious "trading of stamps."

The story of Martin will demonstrate what I mean. Martin was an executive as renowned for his emotional outbursts as for his business skills. His outbursts were so extreme that the CEO grew concerned about employee grievances. When I coached Martin, it was clear he did not suffer fools. In his eyes, his comapny hired a lot of fools. Anytime someone did not do as he told them in the operating room or did not appear focused on his patients, he subconsciously filed that event in his brain under the offender's name. Whenever an offender's file was full, he would unload it on them in a public place. Until we discussed his outbursts, he was unaware of his mental file cabinet.

Martin decided on a new strategy. He placed an actual box in his office, which he named the "Stupid Box." This served three purposes: 1) to keep him conscious of his tendency toward outbursts, 2) to move the file from his subconscious to his conscious thoughts, and 3) to provide a moment to pause and consider how to handle the matter so it would not back up on him.

Once we become conscious of our emotional life, it has a lot to teach us. Some emotions will tell us we're too stirred up to take immediate action and need a brief cooling-off period first. That does not mean we are avoiding our feelings. Rather, it means we are listening to what our emotions are telling us, and responding to our emotional need for reflection and patience. That is the beginning of emotional mastery.

Beliefs Lead to Emotions

Although your emotions are reactions to stimuli, the question of which emotions come up in response to particular events is a reflection of what you believe those events mean. Let's say you believe you *are* your work. Then if you lose your job, you'll likely feel fear because you perceive your survival to be at stake. If you judge this fear as weakness and repress it, you'll probably experience anger, a common response when we are thwarted from expressing ourselves. This can lead to derailing behavior. Build up enough steam this way, and you'll likely lash out at whoever's available.

If, on the other hand, you are a person who views your job simply as one aspect of your life, and you know that your inherent value lies in your unique skills and qualities, then your emotional response to losing your job will probably be a lot different. You might even view this loss as an opportunity to explore a whole new path for yourself.

How you feel in any situation corresponds with what you believe about yourself and the situation. Master your beliefs, and you'll master your emotions.

How do you master beliefs? This is what self-awareness is about. If you lose a client and you feel fear, don't deny the emotion. Instead, acknowledge it and ask what it's telling you. If it's telling you that losing one client will ruin your reputation, take that belief out for a walk. Ask yourself what *reputation* means to you, what is involved in building a reputation, what is involved in losing one, and most importantly, how you developed your ideas about reputation in the first place. You'll likely discover that your beliefs are hooked into stories from your past. Once you know your stories, you can reframe them to tell yourself a new story about *reputation*.

You will always be you. So if your first emotional reaction to losing a client is fear, that fear might always come up for you. However, you can choose not to act on the first emotion that comes up. Instead, you can reflect on your new story, which may refocus your thoughts and lead to new emotions. With practice, you too may begin to see through the loss to the opportunity. By mastering your beliefs, you will begin to master your emotions.

Emotional Choices Can Be Good Choices

There's no doubt about it: emotions affect decisions. Yet it's still a common belief that effective decision-making requires rational thinking absent of emotion. While many leaders believe they lean on logic for their decisions, the truth is that all decisions rely heavily on feelings. Accepting this reality is a big step in putting leaders at greater choice.

When we use pure logic to make decisions, we seek to exclude emotions, relying on such methods as conducting or studying research, listing pros and cons, prioritizing goals, even making mathematical calculations. The foundation of such decisions is utility: assessing the value of each option by assigning criteria to the desired outcome. This can yield data that's helpful in making decisions. The catch is that new ideas are difficult to measure by preexisting criteria.

New ideas and inventions often call for leaps of logic, or leaps of faith, that cannot be measured because the yardsticks for them do not yet exist. Such innovations are what human successes are built on. Innovations that include risk require us to rely heavily on intuition, which largely reveals itself via emotions. Sometimes a decision simply feels right, all apparent logic to the contrary.

We tend to lean more on emotions in decision-making when we're under pressure to choose quickly. A completely emotional decision can happen almost instantaneously. It takes longer—at least 0.1 seconds—for the rational cortex to get going.[27] The reactive, subconscious decisions you encounter in heated arguments or life-threatening situations are largely driven by emotion. At such moments, people often ignore logic or build their logical arguments on false premises. In slower decision-making, people typically consider a series of logical criteria, and then invite emotion back into the process when they make their final choice.

Neuroscientist Antonio Damasio studied decision-making in people who had received brain injuries that had one specific effect: the part of the brain that generates emotions was damaged. The interesting common denominator Damasio found was that their ability to make decisions was seriously impaired. They could logically describe what they should be doing, but in practice they found it difficult to make decisions about which tasks to prioritize at work, how to spend money, where to live, even what to eat. They had the biggest problem with decisions that had pros and cons on both sides, such as *Shall I have the fish or the beef?* In any situation in which they did not have enough rational criteria for a decision, they were unable to make one.[28]

Regardless of the value of logically weighing information, at the point when a person comes to a decision, emotions play a critical role. Even when we believe we're making logical decisions, the final choice is arguably always based on emotion. This is why we talk about decisions that "feel right." When our logical choices are mistaken, we often have the feeling that "something is wrong" long before the results come in.

Emotions may well be signals from the subconscious that tell us which choices are the best to fulfill the beliefs, values, and goals that are important to us.

Damasio also looked at research in which a subject's brain was wired to recorders and the subject was asked to simply press a red button at any time. The notion was that if the conscious mind was in charge of decisions, then electrical activity would start in that part of the brain first, but if the subconscious was in charge of decisions, then the change would be seen there first. The answer Damasio discovered: when it comes to decisions, our subconscious is in the driver's seat.

A self-aware leader accepts that his or her subconscious is largely in charge of their choices, and instead of trying to figure a way around that, learns to trust it. Emotions stem from the subconscious, so we don't choose whether or not to let them into our decisions. *They are there from the start.* This makes it incumbent on the aware leaders to get to know and trust their emotions.

When we know what prompts our emotions,
we prepare ourselves to make better choices.

Progressive leaders have fluid emotional lives, responding honestly to what their emotions tell them. Staying in touch with their emotions primes their subconscious minds to intuit better choices for themselves and their organizations.

Check in on Your Emotions

Are you a master of your emotions? If you attempt to avoid emotions, you run the risk of becoming either robot-like or explosive, both of which are off-putting to others. If you feel your emotions but avoid expressing them, you may falsify your relationships, undermine your health, and delay your personal development. To get a better sense of where you are in your journey to emotional mastery, check the following statements that typically apply to you:

- I know what I want and take action to make it happen.
- I think before acting and have control over my behavior.
- I am self-reliant and take responsibility for my actions.
- I am patient.
- I connect with others in a cooperative way.
- I genuinely care about others and demonstrate compassion.
- I am honest and live by my principles.
- I seek moderation in all things.
- I follow through on commitments, even when it is difficult.
- I am humble and am willing to admit, "I was wrong. I'm sorry."

The qualities above indicate emotional mastery. Please don't use the list to judge yourself as either a failure or a master. Mastery is a journey, not a destination. The checked boxes indicate aspects of your emotional life worth leaning into as you make decisions. The unchecked boxes indicate places in your life worth observing to discover new opportunities for growth.

As you move in the direction of emotional mastery, your relationships will benefit. To gauge how well you leverage your emotional life to create healthy, beneficial, productive relationships, check the following boxes that typically apply to you:

- I understand how to communicate appropriately for each relationship and situation.
- I clarify assumptions and correct mistakes.
- I weigh and balance issues when things go wrong and seek fairness in solutions.
- I build and maintain friendships.
- I collaborate with teams to achieve shared goals.
- I inspire and lead others.

The checked boxes in that last list indicate the qualities that serve you best in your relationships with others. Lean on those. As for the rest, know that these are areas where you need to practice your social networking skills. Emotional mastery will make it easier to build all of your relationships, as you discover how the way you deal with emotions can impact others.

Anticipating Triggers and Jerks

Becoming aware of my emotional life has helped me get a handle on one of my old derailing behaviors. I used to ignore my emotions until I exploded, laying into whatever unlucky people happened to be in my path. Today I monitor my emotional states, especially around people who trigger me. One of the basic tools I use to help me stay on top of that is *anticipation*.

I remember working at an advertising agency with the worst hire I ever made. Let's call him Wayne. Wayne was a self-centered, untrustworthy manipulator who worked in the shadows against the team. I'm pretty sure nobody liked Wayne, but for a while we had no choice except to deal with him. I knew I could not effectively lead my team if I blew up at meetings, and I also knew that Wayne could easily set me off. So I anticipated that emotional trigger and did one simple thing to prepare for team meetings: I wrote Wayne's name on a little card and set it down on my legal pad where nobody could see it but me. Whenever I felt irritation building in me, I looked at the card and pulled myself back. "Oh, right," I thought. "That's just Wayne being Wayne. Nothing I can do about that. Don't let who he is influence who I am."

My emotional reaction to Wayne was still there. I still felt irritation and frustration. But I responded with the appropriate action, which in this case was to take no action. This allowed me to be more present, aware, and available for the team as a whole. If I had worked with Wayne longer, a situation might have come up when it would have been appropriate to confront him, although not at a team meeting. The important thing was that I accepted my feelings and moved on. That is emotional fluidity, and it allows me to be a better leader.

The Frustrating Emotion of Frustration

To experience life is to feel a gamut of emotions. When we judge feelings, we often decide joy is good and frustration is bad. Emotions are neither good nor bad. Such values only come into play when we choose what to do with emotions. Frustration is simply a reaction to not having something we want. If we had everything we wanted, we would have no motivation to pursue goals that bring us joy. So the path to joy often requires us to first experience frustration. Accepting the usefulness of all emotions, including frustration, keeps things in perspective.

Consider Carol, a client of mine who discovered that even getting what we want can lead to frustration. Carol was excited to be chosen as Chief Human Resource Officer at her new company, a biotech firm, but she faced immediate frustration. Her biggest challenge was that she was new to the industry. One of her responsibilities was executive onboarding, yet her frustration made it difficult to make her own transition onboard. She had envisioned exciting changes, but she ran into unexpected obstacles that made it hard to achieve goals at the pace to which she was accustomed. She made decisions that had worked well in her previous jobs, but which did not work in her new organization. Her peers offered to answer any questions she might have, but because she did not know what she did not know, she didn't know what questions to ask.

There was nothing wrong with Carol's emotional reaction. Frustration is a normal response to obstacles, and it can be a great motivator. But first Carol needed to face her feelings.

When results frustrate us, the causes can be internal, external, or both. One internal cause of frustration can be disappointment in ourselves when we believe we are not getting what we want due to real or imagined personal deficiencies. Another internal source is the realization that we have two competing goals or two conflicting sets of values. Think about the conflicts that arise when work and family are both important to you.

External causes of frustration involve conditions outside our control, such as people who don't come through on commitments or unavailability of resources. Think about how frustrated you get when you have to wait for a decision from people who cannot make up their minds, or when a project is delayed because you have no access to resources.

Sometimes we get frustrated with ourselves for being frustrated.

We need a more fruitful approach to frustration. We can begin by accepting frustration without judgment, listening to what it has to tell us about what we're not achieving, and letting it motivate us to find solutions and take action. When we trust ourselves to bear frustration, learn from it, and use it to improve our lives, we discover our power to transcend obstacles.

To help you in your practice of emotional mastery, try the following mindful moment involving frustration:

MINDFUL MOMENT #3
FRUSTRATION AND THE PATH TO EMOTIONAL MASTERY

1. For two weeks keep a list of frustrations that arise.
2. At least once a day, pause, reflect, and write down the frustrations you faced that day.

3. At the end of two weeks, review your list.
4. Without judgment, notice those frustrations that repeat and those that are novel to you.
5. Ask yourself if there's a pattern to your frustrations. If so, can you anticipate those frustrations and create strategies for alternative responses?
6. Consider whether any novel frustrations have anything new to teach you about where you might grow next in your goals.
7. Remember, you have a choice over whether to act on a frustration or let it go. Each choice will have lessons for you that deepen your understanding of yourself and your values.
8. Acknowledge yourself for taking an important step toward self-awareness. Not everyone searches for the meaning of emotions. You are one step closer to emotional mastery.

It is impossible to eliminate all obstacles in life, so there's no point in compounding your frustrations by battling them. Embracing frustration as an opportunity for growth is one of the ways we increase our trust in our own resourcefulness.

"If you so choose, every mistake can lead to greater understanding and effectiveness. If you so choose, every frustration can help you to be more patient and more persistent."

— Ralph Marston

Manage Your Emotions

Over many years of coaching executives, I've found a few insights useful to help each of them blaze their own trail to emotional mastery. Here are a few practices that may help you to not only manage your emotions, but also to harness your emotional energy as a leadership tool:

Earn rather than defend: Instead of growing defensive when people challenge you, focus on something other than your differences. Instead of protecting your position or forcing your viewpoint on others, ask yourself what else is going on here. The thing that's upsetting them might not be about you. Even if it is, the old saying is true, "When you change someone's point-of-view against their will, you've never truly changed them." The moment you lose self-control, you've lost the battle. However, if you manage your emotions, ask questions, and show interest, you open yourself to the possibility of a calm, enlightening discussion.

Acknowledge rather than agree: It's possible to acknowledge that someone has a different viewpoint without agreeing. Sometimes the more strongly someone disagrees with us, the more adamant we become about convincing them we're right. Ask yourself, "How important is it?" If the answer comes down to personal pride, let it go. Acknowledge the other person's views as well as your own, and then allow the conversation to drift to another topic. Your respect for other people's right to differ is more likely to win respect than your effort to change their minds.

Express your emotions: Expressing empathy and sharing emotional honesty are two hallmarks of the aware leader. Everyone you work with knows you're human, and there's no percentage in pretending otherwise. When you honestly share your strengths and weaknesses, trials and triumphs with those around you, you forge a more personal connection. Never forget that people follow those they like. While your primary concern at the office might not be to make friends, opening up to your team will help develop trust and loyalty between you, which will increase your effectiveness as a leader.

Voice your integrity: Emotional self-control does not mean being silent about your values. Just the opposite. When someone crosses your boundaries, the question is not how to avoid confronting a difficult subject, but instead how to share your concerns while keeping a level head. If you can do this, others will see you as a person to turn to when the truth needs telling. By showing others you are a person of integrity, you will bolster your reputation as a leader. Respect follows those whose "yes" means "yes" and whose "no" means "no."

Tactfully handle the negative: Negative people will always be around, people who complain, create unnecessary confrontation, and lack self-control. If their contribution does not outweigh their damaging attitude, and if you have authority, you might want to transfer them to positions more suited to their talents and needs. Otherwise, your best approach may be to focus on the positives they bring to the table, acknowledge their opinions and quickly move on. Most importantly, anticipate ways they might trigger you. This can make it easier for you to choose responses that are grounded in emotional steadiness.

As you strive to master your emotional life, remember: your feelings are uncontestable. They're not open to dispute. If you "feel bad" and you or someone else tries to convince you otherwise, that is not productive. We master emotions by accepting them, all of them, not just the ones we like. Emotions are central to the human experience. If you wish to lead humans to success, then emotions are an experience you need to embrace.

A WORD TO THE AWARE LEADER:

When dealing with people, remember you are not dealing with creatures of logic, but with creatures of emotion.

—Dale Carnegie

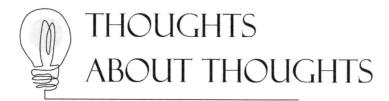

SEVEN

THOUGHTS ABOUT THOUGHTS

Bad News Brain

Do you ever feel as if a news report keeps running in your head and all the news is bad? If so, you're not alone. The human brain has developed to be hypersensitive to negative input. That's not all bad. It often keeps us out of harm's way. You're here today because your ancestors heeded their brains' negative warnings and did not get eaten by wild beasts or competing tribes. Unfortunately our brain is a little too good at this, calling up our errors of the past over and over again, blaming us repeatedly as it tries to protect us from repeating our mistakes.

The brain's negative bias also plays a powerful role in our executive lives, where negative thoughts often eat away at productivity, creativity, and decisiveness. Many executives I work with spend so much time thinking about how to prevent failure that they forget to focus on creating success. In the book *The Progress Principle*, Harvard Business School professor Teresa Amabile and psychologist Steven Kramer point out that negative setbacks are three times more powerful in affecting human motivation than positive progress.[29] We just find it easier to remember the bad things that happen.

It can be helpful to remind yourself that, in reality, most life experiences are neutral until you personalize them and give them positive or negative meaning.

By the time I encounter executives, most have transitioned into their largest roles to-date without ever having made a connection between their early life experiences and how they lead now. To help them make those connections, I start by identifying the behaviors they engage in that are most likely to hinder their success.

LEADERS UNAWARE OF HOW THEIR PERSONAL HISTORY AFFECTS THEM MIGHT:

- be excessively introspective, vigilant, or worried about their performance.
- be overly self-critical.
- take criticism personally.
- be their own worst enemy.
- act intense, edgy, or stressed.
- exhibit boundary issues.
- fear being "found out" as less qualified than they're expected to be.

Despite the above internal thoughts and external behaviors, these executives have gotten to where they are through years of successful efforts. The key to this paradox is typically their vigilance. They became high achievers as a result of an overly active response to constant negative thoughts warning them to watch out for looming failure. The problem is that such vigilance won't take them all the way, and might even derail them in the end.

Vigilance can lead to exhaustion, anxiety, or overly emotional behavior. That behavior may be aggressive, dependent, or withdrawing. All those reactions are potential derailers.

In my work with executives, the goal is not to stop every negative thought. Instead I encourage them to unveil the history behind such thoughts. With increased awareness of our personal histories, we can name where negative thoughts come from, giving us power to redirect them. Consider the difference between these related thoughts: "I'm horrible at this task" versus "I'm having that old childhood thought about being bad at everything." Reframing a thought can move you away from having no choice to having a choice: "What will I do with this thought?"

Thoughts Are Not Feelings

It's easy to confuse thoughts and feelings, but aware leaders learn to identify the difference. Separating thoughts from feelings, and understanding the way each influences the other, is an important component of self-awareness. Here's one way that people get confused:

Someone asks you, "How do you feel about global warming?"

Maybe you reply, "It's devastating our planet." That's not a feeling. That's a thought.

If you want to relate a feeling, you might say, "I feel worried," or "I feel angry."

It further complicates the matter if the person asking the question didn't consider the difference either. When communicating thoughts and feelings, it can be helpful to clarify: "Let me make sure I understand; were you looking for my opinion, or my emotional reaction?"

Thoughts are mental cognitions: ideas, opinions, and beliefs. They include the perspectives we bring to any experience, coloring our viewpoint as we decide how to act. Thoughts come from the brain's cerebral cortex, which rationally processes information. Thoughts help us make sense of our world, our actions, and the actions of others.

On the other hand, emotions are the flow and experience of feelings, which can be responses to external stimuli or responses to thoughts. Some of these responses are incredibly quick. The amygdala is part of the limbic system, the brain's primitive emotion center. The amygdala is all about survival, and it triggers emotions faster than we're consciously aware. While it takes around 300 milliseconds for you to become consciously aware of a disturbing event, the amygdala reacts to it within 20 milliseconds! Awareness of this mechanism enables you to plan for and mitigate its potential ill effects, and to recover your peace of mind.

We subconsciously recognize emotions by the way our bodies react. When we feel fear, our heart rate might increase, adrenaline might give us an urge to run, or a hollow feeling in our stomach might make us freeze. When we feel joy, we might feel energetic, our nerves might tingle, or we might feel a desire to laugh. Thoughts do not have this physical component.

Even though thoughts are not feelings, thoughts do have a direct impact on how you feel. Thoughts are also easier to change than feelings. That's important to know because, if you change your thoughts, you can change your feelings. For example, if you invite yourself to think about all the blessings in your life, this can lead to joy. On the other hand, if you suggest to yourself to think about all your mistakes, that might lead to embarrassment. This is not to say you should never ponder your mistakes. All feelings have value in guiding us to better choices.

When we confuse thoughts and feelings,
we're likely out of touch with our feelings.

By being aware of our thoughts, we can shift them in directions that lead to emotions that are more useful to us. For example, at a morning presentation you might need to focus more on confident thoughts that give you joyful energy. On the other hand, if you're procrastinating about writing a marketing proposal, you might feel more motivated by your anger over the thought that a competitor outsmarted you last time—*I'm not letting them beat me again! Better get cracking!*

Thoughts and feelings constantly influence each other. A thought like *My effort to motivate team members never gets them moving* might generate an emotion like anger, which can lead to other thoughts, like: *My team must be lazy.*

Thoughts often arise on their own, but we can send them in a new direction. On the heel of the thought, *My effort to motivate team members never gets them moving,* you could ask yourself questions, like: *How do I know they're not moving? Have I been clear about what I want? Was there a time I did motivate them?* Such questions might lead to a new thought: *On our last project, we finished ahead of schedule,* which might lead to a feeling of confidence, which might yield another thought: *My team seems more excited when I give them clear objectives.* The new train of thought offers you new choices.

By the same token, emotions often arise on their own, leading to related thoughts. We can also interrupt that process by offering ourselves new thoughts to consider. This can shift our emotional state, helping us create a new train of thought.

It's critical to understand how thoughts and feelings influence each other. Together they inform our choices, which dictate who we become. Some causal chains of thoughts, feelings, and actions become vicious cycles: we believe we're incompetent, so we lose confidence, so we act indecisively, leading to poor results, bolstering our belief in our incompetence.

Bad things happen to everyone, and it's unrealistic to think we'll be positive every minute of the day. But when we are aware of the world around us, our emotional reactions to that world, and the thoughts we entertain about it, we have the choice to pursue a new line of thinking that has the power to carry us to new emotions and actions. The mark of the aware leader is not how perfectly we arrange our world so that nothing ever takes us off track, but rather how strong we are at responding with self-awareness, and how willing we are to choose more useful thoughts.

How Joyce's Thoughts Threatened to Derail Her

I met Joyce when she became the COO for a small software company on the East Coast. It was her largest role ever, and she was determined to be successful. Her industry was in the midst of vast change, change that was anticipated but not clearly identified. She was busy overseeing daily operational needs, implementing change initiatives, and reading intuitive tea leaves to predict future change. The inherent stress in all that would have the power to impact anyone's thinking.

Joyce was feeling challenged to keep up with the loads of information streaming to her via email. She often attended meetings where she was surprised by unexpected information from team members. When she asked them to clarify, she heard responses like, "I sent an email to you about this last week." Her thoughts often jumped from, "I should have read that email" to "I cannot keep up" to "I'm disorganized" to "I'm going to fail."

Every time Joyce's mind churned like that, she was no longer fully present. When she ruminated about failing, her guidance of meetings became less effective. She was unable to synthesize information so she could draw conclusions, choose actions, or offer clear direction to her team. She was stuck in her head. Joyce's thoughts often churned for days until she concluded, "Great executives don't let this happen. They deal with pressure and change, but I don't."

Like Joyce, we each have a schema of preconceived ideas that organizes the information in our heads. Like most of us, Joyce's preconceived ideas sprang from childhood experiences. Her parents had demanded perfection, and she had worked diligently to please. Even though she was now an adult in a position of power, she could not shake the habit of trying to please Mom and Dad. This resulted in self-talk that reminded her she must be perfect. When she wasn't, she felt like a child letting down Mom and Dad.

If you pay attention to your internal life when you feel challenged, you will find that patterns emerge in the thoughts, emotions, and personal stories that arise. This influences the way you pay attention to the world around you. This becomes your scheme for organizing information, which is a nonstop process because the brain works 24/7 churning out thoughts and feelings. If you don't develop awareness of your schema, it can prompt you to engage in unconscious behavior patterns that don't serve you, or anyone else for that matter.

Your thoughts and feelings from moment to moment are filtered through the default settings you developed early in life to survive, get along, and get ahead.

Many thoughts that threaten to derail us come from our experiences with childhood caregivers. Some derailing thoughts are quotes of things parents, siblings, or peers said to us: "You're so clumsy!" or "You never think!" Sometimes derailing thoughts spring from positive origins, moments when grownups provided us with ethical guideposts, like: "Anything worth doing is worth doing well," or "If you want other kids to play with you, you have to share." Children don't know how to prioritize such ideas, and memory distorts them. Since cognitive abilities don't fully develop until our mid-twenties, imagine how many of your habitual thoughts no longer serve you!

In coaching sessions with Joyce, I encouraged her to objectively observe her thoughts and feelings during meetings. This practice helped her notice a problem she hadn't considered: she was rushing from one meeting to another with no time to pause and regroup, which exacerbated her downward spiral of thoughts and emotions. She would rush to the next meeting still thinking about what had happened in the last one. As a result, she was not fully present at meetings, her mind racing with thoughts like, "How will I ever get all those things done?"

Joyce needed to recharge between meetings. Like most executives, she had little time to spare. We talked about what sorts of things bring her joy. Her face lit up when she talked about her grandson and showed me photos of him on her iPhone. We came up with an idea for her to pull up a picture of him while walking to meetings. This grounded her in her values around family, took her mind off the spin cycle of to-dos, and calmed her thoughts. She felt more present at meetings, which helped her more effectively exchange information with her team, which built confidence in her ability to handle her responsibilities. This simple practice strengthened Joyce's observing self. She improved her ability to notice and diffuse negative thoughts sooner and developed additional strategies to redirect the thoughts before they spiraled out of control. All of her strategies focused prioritizing her values over frenzy.

Self-Talk

You can observe your own schema within the words and language you use during self-talk. It is critical for leaders to pay attention to their self-talk. Think of a recent challenge you faced. When it happened, what did you say to yourself *about* yourself, either out loud or silently? That is self-talk. Think in terms of Joyce's self-talk, which moved from *imperfect* to *incapable* to *disorganized* to *failure* to *bad executive*. What trajectory did your thoughts follow?

According to psychotherapist Russ Harris, leading expert in Acceptance and Commitment Therapy (ACT), there are three kinds of thoughts: 1) helpful, 2) problematic, and 3) minimally important.[30] Let's take a look at each of these sorts of thoughts one at a time:

1. **Helpful Thoughts:** Helpful thoughts allow you choose your responses to events instead of heedlessly reacting. Helpful thoughts align with your values, provide useful information, and link to other thoughts that can inform your choices. Helpful thoughts remind you of the positives you bring to a situation: skills, knowledge, or attributes; memories of similar situations in which you've succeeded in the past; or what trusted friends, colleagues, and mentors have told you works for you.

Helpful thoughts develop your confidence by building your awareness of all you bring to the table.

Helpful thoughts give you feedback on emotions, providing data on those emotions to give you more choices about how to respond to a situation. For example, if you feel nervous before a presentation, helpful thoughts inform you where that comes from: maybe it's the normal edge that comes with presenting a new idea to a group, or maybe you're unprepared. Even if the latter is the case, now that you know where it's coming from you have choices, such as: ask for help, shorten your talk, shift the purpose of the session, or acknowledge what you need to do to prepare next time.

Helpful thoughts provide essential information about our changing emotional states. Those emotions, pleasant or unpleasant, become indicators for effective action.

2. **Problematic Thoughts:** Problematic thoughts are made up of negative and/or illogical self-talk. We engage in problematic thinking when we put ourselves down, criticize ourselves for errors, doubt our abilities, expect failure, or fear the future. Negative thinking paralyzes mental skills and damages confidence, which harms our performance.

The problem with avoiding problematic thoughts is that they tend to dart into our consciousness without warning and dart out again, doing damage without us recognizing their significance. People rarely challenge momentary thoughts, so they rarely discover when such thoughts are incorrect preconceptions. This increases their injurious effect.

It's all too easy to embrace problematic thoughts as reality. To help you recognize the seriousness of this trap, try this exercise first introduced by Russ Harris.

AN EXERCISE IN DISENGAGING FROM PROBLEMATIC THOUGHTS (RUSS HARRIS):

Imagine that your hands are your thoughts. When you reach the end of this paragraph, put this book down and hold your hands side-by-side, palms open, like the pages of an open book. Then slowly raise your hands toward your face until they are covering your eyes. Look around you through the gaps between your fingers. Notice how this affects your view of the world. Please do this exercise now before reading further.

Imagine what it would be like to go around all day with your hands covering your eyes in that manner. How much would you miss? How would it limit your ability to respond to the world around you? This is similar to the way we restrict ourselves when we get caught up in problematic thoughts. We lose contact with many aspects of our here-and-now experience. Thoughts have such a huge influence over our actions that our ability to act effectively is significantly reduced.

When you reach the end of this paragraph, once again cover your eyes with your hands, but this time slowly lower them from your face. Notice how much easier it is to connect with the world around you. Please do this now before reading further.

That is how open you can be to the world if you disengage from problematic thinking.

You might be thinking, *I understand that problematic thoughts obscure my clear view of the world, but if they come up unbidden, how can I stop them?* Recognizing problematic thought-traps helps. When they come up, ask yourself questions about what is actually happening right now, bringing yourself back in touch with the reality of the present moment.

BEWARE OF PROBLEMATIC THOUGHT-TRAPS:

- Trying to master your fate by predicting catastrophe (catastrophizing)
- Assuming you know what others think about you
- Thinking you should be appreciated by all, or that this is even possible
- Thinking the problems you encounter are too big to tackle
- Holding onto outdated thoughts and personal stories that no longer represent you
- Comparing yourself with others
- Defining yourself in negative terms
- Assuming your negative thoughts represent reality
- Assuming you are your thoughts
- Believing that either you or someone else must be to blame for your problems

3. **Minimally Important Thoughts:** Not all thoughts are helpful or problematic. Most are minimally important, inane, or undemanding. Thoughts like *feed the dog, water the yard, brush your teeth, start the car, drink water, select a movie, daydream,* require no effort, skill, or attention. They have little relevance to our values, decisions, or goals. Minimally important thoughts are easily managed. We can choose to dart away at any time.

Even thoughts that are helpful or problematic are not all equally important. The most important thoughts to be aware of are those that either move you toward or away from your values. Thoughts that affect your goals, your ability to be present, and your ability to create a meaningful life are also important. Accepting these important thoughts, whether they're helpful or problematic, is a crucial step in self-awareness.

You might be surprised that I deem it important to accept problematic thoughts. After all, you do want to reduce your focus on them. But you cannot disconnect from problematic thoughts unless you first accept their existence. Even after you disconnect from them, new ones will arise. You're only human. Awareness and acceptance of all your thoughts is your best avenue to prioritizing which thoughts to give your attention.

Effective leaders recognize that thoughts are not orders. Just because you have a thought does not mean you must act on it. Thoughts are just words in your mind. They represent your opinions, beliefs, and ideas about reality, but they are *not* reality itself. As you see thoughts for what they are, you sift through them with more awareness, opening yourself to more choices.

Unhooking From Problematic Thoughts

Although we cannot control random thoughts, we can control our behavior in response to them. A simple example of this is one we teach children: that they can have angry thoughts that make them want to hit someone, but they can choose not to. "Use your words," we say. It's good advice for grownups too.

Many of us grew up among parents, teachers, and peers who admonished us to "stop being a pessimist," or "change your attitude." Today colleagues and friends might talk to us about putting out "positive energy" or using "positive thinking." A positive attitude is useful. However, when we worry that certain thoughts are bad, or that people will judge us for them, we create a bigger problem. The moment you tell yourself, "Don't think about that," you're already thinking about it. Then your next thought is likely to be, "Oh no, I'm thinking negative thoughts that might cause negative results." This can paralyze you. Psychological research shows that when we try to regulate unwanted thoughts, they tend to intensify.

Paradoxically, the easiest way to defeat negative thoughts is to accept them. Controlling them is not possible. They arise on their own, prompted by default settings. Acceptance is the quickest way to let them pass so you can move on. By accepting all thoughts without judgment, you open yourself to a more complete menu of information to help you make effective choices. Once you accept problematic thoughts, you can improve your skills at unhooking from them.

The next time you get stuck in a problematic thinking trap, try this mindfulness exercise:

MINDFUL MOMENT #4:
AWARENESS OF PROBLEMATIC THOUGHTS

1. Take out a notepad and pen.
2. Write down this heading: Problematic Thoughts My Mind Is Telling Me.
3. Now list all of your current thoughts, no matter how minimal you think they are.
4. Put your pen down and step away from your notepad and desk. Tell yourself, These thoughts are merely words. They are not me. I am much more than these thoughts.
5. Sense the distance between you and those problematic thoughts. Physically step back even farther, putting more distance between you and the unhelpful thoughts.
6. How do the thoughts feel now?

When you don't have a notepad handy, or cannot stop to write, you can still use this exercise to unhook from problematic thoughts. You simple need to pause and acknowledge your negative thoughts. Keep it simple: *My mind is having the thought that* _____.
This conscious choice to reframe your thoughts gets you into the detached mode of the observing self. That process alone can unhook the thought, freeing you to turn to new thoughts as you consider your choices about how to respond in the situation before you.

As you accept problematic thoughts and create objective distance from them, you will see them simply as information to consider, or to set aside, when choosing a course of action.

How Kelly's Thoughts Nearly Derailed Her

Kelly worked for an energy company in the Mid-Atlantic. When I served as her leadership coach she was a divisional vice president, identified as a high-potential executive. Kelly took the "high-potential executive" designation with a grain of salt. She thought of herself as an accountant, not an engineer. "Only engineers make it to the senior executive team, and I am *not* an engineer," she told herself over and over. She was hooked on this omnipresent belief.

I worked with Kelly on a series of assessments, which indicated that she tended to be self-doubting, to put unnecessary pressure on herself, and to grow irritable under pressure. She tended to admit to more personal shortcomings than was necessary or realistic.

When I presented her with that information, she paused to reflect and then shared a story about her relationship with her mother. Kelly's mother frequently criticized her while also offering inconsistent criteria for approval. What's more, her mother hovered over her, preventing her from developing confidence in her abilities. As a result, Kelly always felt defective.

That became Kelly's default setting, creating a thought chain that led to: *I Am Not An Engineer*. Her ability to recognize that she was holding on to outdated thoughts was an "aha" moment. We identified her *I Am Not An Engineer* belief as a problematic thought. She worked on her awareness of that thought as only a thought. Then she challenged herself to let in other information about herself, including all the ways in which she was not *de*fective but *ef*fective.

Kelly developed strategies to recognize her internal dialogue, which she named *I Am Not An Engineer* thoughts. Her internal script was inconsistent with information she received from peers, direct reports, and supervisors. She learned to accept *I Am Not An Engineer* thoughts, and to view them as only one of many pieces of information to choose from. Reframing her *I Am Not An Engineer* thoughts did not make them disappear, but they did fade to background noise.

Kelly started a new thought process with this question: "What would I need to do to be promoted to senior executive?" It was a fact that she was *not* an engineer and she accepted that becoming one was not the answer. The answer lay in discovering that it was not necessary for her to become an engineer to be the effective leader of a team, even a team of engineers.

Within one year Kelly was promoted. She has since been recognized among "Women Worth Watching," and has received the Shattered Glass Ceiling Award.

As you practice self-awareness, you too will discover repeating mantras of problematic thoughts. Everyone has them. Don't fear those thoughts. Congratulate yourself for your self-knowledge, because now that you know what your problematic thoughts are, you have the choice to unhook from them. You no longer need to let them take charge of your life.

When to Listen to Intuition

Somewhere between thoughts and feelings lies intuition. Intuition can provide powerful information. How do we know when to listen to intuition and when to take a more logical approach? We don't. Leadership is not about knowing it all. Risk is always a factor. Intuition is most useful when we see it simply as another piece of the puzzle.

Say I interview someone for a position who has all the right qualifications and gives all the right answers, yet I intuit that he or she is wrong for the job. That's not necessarily a sign that I should *not* hire the person, but it may be a sign that I need more information.

I need to validate my intuition with facts. As I research the theoretical interviewee, I might discover new information or new thoughts. Maybe this person reminds me of someone I had a problem with in the past. Is it merely the sound of the voice or color of the hair, which I can dismiss as irrelevant? Or is it a red flag in the conversation? Maybe this person acts like the hero of every story, forever rescuing colleagues from their own incompetence. In that case, following my intuition might save me from a hire who builds personal reputation at the expense of others.

Sometimes intuition leads us to more information about ourselves. Maybe we need to discover why we react the way we do to certain people or situations.

Once we have all the information we need to make a decision, the final choice still requires a leap of faith. Intuition can help us make that leap. When two choices seem equally weighted, intuition can help us get off the dime. Sometimes intuition comes as a culmination of all the information we have been gathering, consciously and subconsciously, the result of our brain's ability to process on multiple levels.

Every piece of information we possess, whether we hold that information as thought, feeling, or intuition, puts us in a place of greater choice. The ability to more clearly identify all our options and confidently choose from among them is the mark of a self-aware leader. It is not in seeing one path, but rather in the ability to see many paths, that the aware leader finds the way to success.

A WORD TO THE AWARE LEADER:

As a single footstep will not make a path on the earth, so a single thought will not make a pathway in the mind. To make a deep physical path, we walk again and again. To make a deep mental path, we must think over and over the kind of thoughts we wish to dominate our lives.

— Henry David Thoreau

EIGHT

THE VALUE
OF VALUES

Your Authentic Self Is True to Your Values

As you invest more energy in following the Ancient Greek maxim, "Know thyself," don't be surprised if you sometimes feel as if you know less about yourself than before. That's a common response when we take a closer look at anything: we first discover what we don't know. For all that we've explored in this book so far, you may have only just begun to figure out who you are. You have learned that knowledge, experience, and skills are great leadership tools, but that they don't define the kind of leader you are. For that, you need to understand your behavior, styles, and preferences. We've talked about behavior, which is about actions, and we've talked about style, which is about personality. Now I'd like to talk about preferences, better known as your values.

To become the most aware leader you can be, you need to identify your core values. Your values form the compass that gives you direction, pointing the way to your purpose and guiding your choices. If you don't develop an awareness of your values, it's like having a compass with no needle. You will have a hard time developing criteria for effective decisions, and may find it difficult to make decisions at all. On the other hand, the more you get to know your values, the more they can motivate and inspire you to make choices that transform your life, the lives of others, and therefore the future of organizations.

"...truth is that which makes a people certain, clear, and strong." — Martin Heidegger

---

All leaders face existential questions at some point: Why am I here? What is the meaning of my life? How can I make a difference? Life is change, so the answers change. In my opinion, that makes our awareness of the questions more important than the answers. How do you act on that awareness? By being true to your authentic self. What is your authentic self? It is who you are when you align your values with your words, actions, self-image, public image, and goals.

Daryl's Dilemma Came Down to Values

A former client reached out to me because he was struggling with a career decision. Daryl was the vice president of compensation and benefits at a national freight company. A competitor was recruiting him with what looked like the perfect offer, a job that promised greater scope, more exciting challenges, and more money. His current job was challenging, but he found some of the challenges irritating. We discussed the decision filters he was using to evaluate the offer: income, career progression, organizational culture, relationships with reports, and the financial stability of the company that was wooing him. When he passed the decision through these filters, he always came up with the same answer: "Take the job."

Still, something gnawed at him.

I couldn't guess what was bothering him, but I had a feeling I knew how he could find out. "Remember, we've talked about key decisions in life needing to be run through the filter of your values. Have you done that?"

"No, I haven't."

"Why don't you add your values to the equation as additional decision filters?"

I suggested he look over the values questionnaire he had completed during our work together, and run through the pros and cons again. The questionnaire, adapted from Kelly Wilson's Valued Living Questionnaire, asks people to rate the following values in order of importance and write a brief definition of what each value means to them:

TEN VALUES FROM KELLY WILSON'S
VALUED LIVING QUESTIONNAIRE:

1. Couples/Intimate Relationships
2. Parenting
3. Family Relations
4. Social Relations
5. Employment
6. Education and Training
7. Recreation
8. Spirituality
9. Citizenship/Community
10. Health/Physical Wellbeing

When you consider your values, creating your own definitions is crucial because we don't all mean the same thing when we name the same values. To one person Social Relations might mean "activities with groups that share our interests," while to another it might mean "spending time visiting with close friends." For one person Recreation might call up images of dining out and bowling, while for another it might call up hiking and travel. Spirituality can mean something very different to a Baptist than to a Buddhist.

By the way, I've noticed that even those people who have never before spent a lot of time pondering their values don't struggle when it comes to defining and ranking them. Deep within each of us lies a sense of what is important to us. Those priorities are shaped by our upbringing, personal experiences, relationships, education, and societal influences.

About a week after I asked Daryl to revisit his values questionnaire, he got back to me. The relief in his voice was clear. "I'm not taking the job!"

He explained what had been gnawing at him. It related to his highest rated values: Parenting and Family Relations. The new job opportunity would have required him to travel four days a week, which would have meant a significant reduction in his role as a father and family man. Taking the job would have meant moving away from his values.

When it comes to values, most choices come down to two options: Will this choice move me toward my values or away from them?

Someone else who also put a high value on Parenting and Family Relations might just as easily have decided to take the job, and for someone else it might have been the right decision. Another guy might have seen the increased money as an opportunity to take better care of his family, and for that other guy two days a week of quality time might have been enough to satisfy his dedication to family, especially if his children were grown or his wife was equally busy with her career. The point is not to judge your values and the way you approach them, but to be honest with yourself about your values and stay true to them.

The more months that went by after Daryl decided to keep his current position, the more joy his decision brought him. Because he was more attuned to the reasons behind his choices, he was able to find more joy and satisfaction at the job he already had. He more strongly felt the connection between his work and its purpose in serving his values. Making a choice had reminded him of all the reasons he had taken the original job in the first place. He reconnected with his purpose, which reenergized his leadership. Daryl's joy increased when he learned that his wife was expecting their second child.

Values and Goals

Every day, executives face decisions that can move them either away from their values or toward their values. Values come from the heart. They are not determined by what you or others think they *should* be but by what is truly meaningful to you. I cannot suggest to you how to select your values. I only want you to understand that values already exist within you. You cannot force yourself to hold a value you do not hold. I definitely don't suggest you fake having a value that others expect. Putting on a false front is a derailing behavior.

Just so we're clear, I'm not saying you should avoid working with people who have different values from yours. If that were a requirement, no organization would ever make it because we all differ in our values to some degree. I do suggest you avoid working with organizations that put you on a path contrary to your values. Within any organization, there are often a variety of paths available, and people with a variety of values on each of those paths.

Values are not goals, though they certainly affect each other. Your values may inform the goals you choose, and your goals may move you toward or away from your values. The difference between goals and values is that goals express your desire for specific results, while values help you judge what is important to you in life. Other people may well pursue the same goals as you, but they often do so based on different values.

Adhering to your values is important to maintaining your authentic personal identity. That does not mean that exploring your values will always lead you toward bliss. This may be one reason so many leaders put off the journey to self-awareness. Sometimes our values make us uncomfortable: our values might remind us that we are not showing up in the world in a way that would make us proud; our values might call upon us to challenge other people; our values might ask us to give up on goals that no longer align with what we stand for. Values require us to do the hard work of balancing *what we want* with *who we want to be*.

Whatever tangible reward you seek in return for reaching any goal, it helps to remember that you can't take it with you. In the end, the only

thing that is absolutely yours is who you are. That doesn't always make choices easier, only clearer.
Miding Your Values

Pursuing a goal is more likely to bring you joy and success if each step you take on the way to that goal aligns with your values.

Although our deepest values tend to be stable over time, they don't have strict limits or boundaries. They can shift. Most of us have slightly different values in our twenties than in our forties. At the start of your career, monetary success and status might be your top priority. Later, striking a balance between work and family might be what you value more. As your definition of success shifts, so do your values. That's why keeping in touch with your values is a lifelong exercise. Revisit them regularly, especially if you feel unsettled and cannot pinpoint why.

Think about a big decision you're facing now or anticipate facing in the near future. What decision filters will you use to guide your choice? Do those filters include your values? Have you spent time clearly defining what your values are? Your goals are about the future, a time that does not yet exist. But your values exist in the present. So to clarify your values, it helps to bring yourself into the present. With that in mind, try the following exercise created by Alfred James, mindfulness coach, advanced student of Eastern philosophy, and author of the *Pocket Mindfulness* blog:[31]

MINDFUL MOMENT #5
A GAME OF FIVES

Start today with a challenge: notice five sensory experiences you usually don't notice or appreciate. I'm talking about anything you hear, see, feel, smell, or taste. For example, you might hear birds singing in a tree, see the way sunlight fills your kitchen, feel your clothes brushing against your skin as you walk to a meeting, smell flowers in the park, or taste the cream cheese on your bagel. As you notice each of these five things, pause and ask yourself:

- What are the connections this thing has with the world?
- How does this thing benefit my life and the lives of others?
- What is this sight, sound, smell, taste, or sensation really like for me?
- What are some of the intricate details I never thought about before?
- What would life be like without this thing?
- What makes this thing amazing?

For each of the five items, spend at least thirty seconds letting your creative mind explore the wonder, impact, and possibilities these usually unnoticed things have on your life. Allow yourself to fall awake into the world and fully experience your environment. As you do so, realize that you are actively discovering what you value, right now!

By becoming aware of who you are, where you are, what you are doing, and how everything in your environment interacts with you, you cultivate a sensory awareness of being. This reduces stress. It tempers the mind, which Buddha once described as filled with drunken monkeys that jump around screeching and carrying on endlessly. Rather than allow yourself to be led by thoughts and feelings which are heavily influenced by memories of the past or concerns about the future, you are returning to the moment and, in so doing, returning to yourself. Once you are fully present, you can more easily bring your values into the decision process.

As aware leaders, we need to bring the language of values alive in every decision-making conversation. The following is a step-by-step process you can use to do that with your whole team:

5 STEPS TO BRING VALUES INTO TEAM DECISIONS:

STEP 1: Appreciate the presence of differing viewpoints. Make sure you are clear about what your perspective is, then take a step back and look around. Do you need to adjust your view to see more clearly? It's helpful to hear how others see things differently, and to identify your biases, assumptions, and missing perspectives.

STEP 2: Listen and talk to others on your team to identify what's at stake. Enter into a discussion to develop a comprehensive list of the values you all hold, both as individuals and as a team, including organizational values, professional values, and personal values. Dig deep. Create a short list of priority values, what I call guiding lights.

STEP 3: Filter decisions through your team's guiding lights. This will clarify which choices align with those priority values. Recognize that values come into play in different ways for different people. Listen to what all the stakeholders believe to be important.

STEP 4: Choose the option that best fits your team's guiding lights. Find the best fit between available options and your priority values by comparing each option against each value. Always take a close look at the potential negative consequences of your choice before committing to action.

STEP 5: For decision-making to be credible, the course of action you choose needs to be communicated clearly to the entire team. The decision process is not complete until you're sure you all get the connection between the choice and the value it represents.

How Maura's Values Improved Her Success

Maura was a successful chief administrative officer for a national services organization when she made a career change that took her to a professional services firm in Florida. Six months into her new job, she felt frustrated: "Every day I just go to work and then go to my damn apartment." When I gave her a Hogan Assessment, it identified that aesthetics were an important value to her. That is to say, engaging in artistic expression was important for her to feel fulfilled. I could see this just by looking at her. She always dressed impeccably from head to toe. She might count pennies on some things, but I don't think I ever saw her wearing an outfit that wasn't worth $10,000, from one-of-a-kind earrings to silk suits to designer shoes.

So I asked Maura about the artistic side of her life. She said she sometimes went to art galleries and concerts. But in her previous city she used to be on the symphony board and a couple of other arts boards, and since she had moved she had not joined a single arts organization.

I said, "Let me tell you what's going to happen, Maura. Six months from now if you're not involved in the arts, not just going to an event now and then but really involved, you're going to quit and it will have nothing to do with your company. You're not unhappy because of work. You're unhappy because when you get off work you're not doing the things you love most."

I have created a Return on Values (ROV) formula, which is not precise math but which will give you an idea of why Maura had a problem. The formula looks something like this:

RETURN ON VALUES FORMULA

ROV > 1 = choice aligned with values = energy source
ROV < 1 = choice not aligned with values = energy drain

Here's the idea: When we align our choices with our values, those choices become a source of energy that can positively impact all areas of our lives. When we don't align our choices with our values, those choices become an energy drain that can negatively impact even those areas of our lives that appear to have little to do with the choice in question.

Maura took that idea to heart. She stayed with her new organization but transferred to a city where she felt more eager to get out and about, where she also had family, and where she got involved in two or three arts organizations. She hit her values on every front. Since then, not only has she stayed on as a successful leader at her company, she is also happy and fulfilled.

Maura made a value-based decision and it worked. Not only did it help her create more energy to bring to her work so that she could be successful, it also put her in a place where she could feel greater joy in her success. The simplicity of her solution is a reminder to all of us to stay awake to our personal needs. Maura did not have to quit her company to increase her success. She simply needed to bring her values more deeply into her daily life.

Even a small shift in the way we pay attention to our values can be a life-changer.

If we reach our goals but they don't make us happy, that's not success. Reaching an external image of success that does not match our internal values can leave us feeling empty. When we're unable to fully experience our achievements, it's time to figure out where we're not lifting ourselves up. By being aware of our values, we increase our power to be at choice in life.

A WORD TO THE AWARE LEADER:

It's not hard to make decisions when you know what your values are.

—Roy E. Disney

NINE

THE POWER OF CHOICE

What We Choose Becomes Who We Are

George Moore wrote in Act IV of his comedy, *The Bending of the Bough*, "The difficulty in life is the choice." I believe he was onto something there. Think about some of the everyday choices we make and how they add up to determine the course of our lives:

DAILY CHOICES CAN CHANGE OUR LIVES

- When we choose to eat unhealthy foods, we choose to be unhealthy. Do we want to be unhealthy?
- When we choose to go the extra mile at work, we choose to be successful. Do we want success?
- When we choose to lash out at an employee, we choose to discourage their engagement. Do we want unengaged employees?
- When we choose to ask ourselves what makes us tick, we choose self-awareness. Do we believe knowing ourselves will make us better leaders?

We always have choices, even in situations that make us feel stuck. When we tell ourselves, "I have no choice," the decision not to even consider other options is in itself a choice. Even when we do nothing, *that* is a choice.

With each choice that presents itself, we either strive to listen to our better judgment, or rationalize acting against our better judgment, or choose to take no notice that we have judgment at all. Acting against our better judgment is called *akrasia*, which comes from a Greek word that means, "lacking command over oneself." Philosopher Donald Davidson said of *akrasia* that we temporarily convince ourselves the worse course of action is *better*. Why? Because we have not made an all-things-considered judgment, but have instead made a decision based only on a subset of possible considerations—only those considerations we're willing to face.

I would like to add a wrinkle to Davidson's view. He assumes we make choices consciously, but modern research indicates we make many choices without thinking, by habit. The key to moving from habit to choice is self-knowledge. When we seek to understand our values, to focus the direction of our thoughts, and to consider our choices in terms of healthy self-interest, we begin to see who we truly are. Becoming aware of who we are allows us to make choices that take into consideration *all* of the relevant information.

Carla was a client of mine who engaged in *akrasia*. She earned an MBA and diligently worked her way into a position as director of research for a consumer products company, but then she stalled her rise up the ladder by making an unconscious choice to avoid being noticed. She was unable to see that she was working against her own self-interest. To understand how she was sabotaging herself, she had to take a closer look at her story.

Carla's parents were Mexican immigrants, and she was the first person in her family to go to college. Her parents still lived in Mexico and relied on her financial success. So did her husband and children. Her husband worked in construction, but his work was intermittent. Carla's education and self-assurance helped make her the leader of her family. She was the one who made the big decisions: about money, home, family, all of it. That leadership role at home sometimes caused her stress that bled into her leadership role at work. The problem was that she knew her family depended on her, so she spent a lot of time in fear of losing her job.

That was probably why, for a long time, she was a different person with her colleagues than with her family. At the office, she was not the decisive leader she was at home. At home she ran it all, but at work she was quiet. The feedback she received from her peers included things like: "You've got to have a point of view," or "You need to speak up more!"

Carla was aware of all that, but her biggest fear would stop her from making a new choice: "What if I say something wrong and lose my job?"

The thing that had never occurred to Carla was that she didn't have to say smart things all the time to be considered an assertive leader. But that was the only way she had thought of to interpret her colleagues' feedback. She had not considered the possibility of other choices.

That's where I stepped in with a question. "What if you didn't have to make strong declarative statements? What if that wasn't the only way to fully participate in a meeting?"

"What would I do then?" she asked.

I said, "In your previous jobs, were you ever in a meeting you were leading and you heard things from your team and you put all of it together and something came to you, and instead of making a declaration you threw out a challenging question? 'I'm hearing all of you say such-and-such, what do you think about this as a possibility?' Have you ever done that?"

"Yes, I used to do that all the time."

"Really? Can you tell me the difference between doing that with your reports in the past and doing it with your peers now? You obviously have the skill, so can you apply it in this new situation? You don't need to be declarative. You can just ask a question. It's a hypothesis. Everyone knows that hypotheses are not proven theories, so the risk is much less."

She gave it a shot and started asking questions at meetings. At her last performance review she was acknowledged for stepping up more with her opinion and being more assertive. She realized she had more than one choice, and she took advantage of that. That one small change in behavior became a big step up for her.

Carla's choice is an excellent option for introverts because they tend to be good listeners. Introverts are more likely to connect the dots and see the big picture than extroverts, who often focus on their next contribution to the conversation. An introvert who listens carefully might choose to jump in with, "Suzy, when you said this, and Joe said this, and this other piece of data came up, I started wondering…" I'm fond of the words "wondering" or "curious," which assert possibility rather than certainty. Rarely will anybody take issue with that sort of open attitude.

Our choices can facilitate success or hinder success. Making conscious choices instead of being at the mercy of our unconscious choices gives us more power to make a difference in our own lives. Gaining this power starts with paying attention to ourselves, to the stories we bring to the table and to what's going on with us in the moment.

What's Going On?

The next time you're about to do something based on the notion that you have no choice, pause for a moment. Engage your observing self for a little nonjudgmental attention to what's going on inside you. Notice what you're thinking. What kind of self-talk are you engaging in? Do you tell yourself things like: "They're doing it to me" or "I have to do this"? Notice also how you're feeling: do you feel the heaviness that comes with sadness or the prickly sensation of fear? Perhaps those sorts of feelings come up when you feel that others are manipulating you, or when you believe they have the power to destroy you.

Knowing what's going on in your mind and body can help you identify what might be triggering you. Perhaps what's making you feel as if you have no choice is a default setting that is operating on inaccurate information. Or perhaps the underlying problem is real but you have shut down before considering all the information. Once you identify what's really bugging you, you have the opportunity to ask yourself a new question:

"What if I had a choice?"

Once you start considering that question, then who you are, what you want, and what you value can come back into play.

Maybe you already realize you do have a choice, but you just don't want to make one. Being at choice is not always a comfortable place to be. What if you make the wrong one? It's not always possible to know which choice is best. But so long as you know who you are and strive to align with your values, you have a much better chance at making choices that make you proud, or at least choices that don't make you ashamed.

When we know our values, become mindful of our thoughts and feelings, and identify our unconscious habits, we expand our awareness to see choices we did not see before. Even if we don't like the choices, we are in a much more powerful position than those who behave like victims, unable to act with a will of their own.

"You can't stop the waves, but you can learn to surf." — Jon Kabat-Zinn

We cannot change the past, the laws of physics, other people, basic human needs, or who we are. We also cannot change those of our own behaviors we fail to acknowledge. On the other hand, we can change what we know, what we do, and what we aspire to. We can most easily change those things when we engage in the task of self-awareness.

Choice Can Transform Your Actions

Dr. William Glasser was a psychiatrist who developed a method of counseling called Reality Therapy, which relied heavily on the human ability to make choices. His Choice Theory is predicated on three main concepts: 1) that everything we can know about humans is based on their behavior, 2) that almost all behavior is chosen, and 3) that our genes drive us to satisfy five basic needs. Those five needs are: survival, love and belonging, power, freedom, and fun. Although mainstream psychiatrists often find Glasser's ideas controversial, they can be instructive in understanding the role of choice in behavior.[32]

One of Glasser's major premises was that, "All behavior is purposeful." He saw behavior as the result of people making the best choices they can to meet their needs based on the resources at their disposal. The resources we use to make choices are primarily: knowledge, experience, skills, behavior, styles, and preferences. In essence, your choices are your attempt to make the world conform to your idea of what will best serve you.

Most of the time, we select behaviors we're familiar with, primarily behaviors that have worked for us before. For example, when I want to energize, one of my behaviors is to actively participate in events involving other people and to take on a lot of different activities. Why do I do that? Because past experience has taught me that being around people pumps me up and that I enjoy energizing other people with my own enthusiasm.

The challenge, and the opportunity, comes when we bump up against a situation for which we do not have habitual behaviors ready, or when we try habitual behaviors and they don't yield positive results. This is when we find it easiest to consider options we never have before, and risk choosing a new behavior. When we become aware of such moments, we do ourselves a favor by pausing to ask: How can I make a new choice that aligns with my values and my style?

Glasser calls the above shift in behavior patterns "reorganizing." We take the knowledge, experiences, skills, behaviors, styles, and preferences available to us in the moment and creatively choose a new behavior. Our new choice might require us to gain new experiences, new skills, or new knowledge. It might require us to embrace a novel behavior, engage in a new style, or consider the possibility of discovering a new preference.

According to Dr. Glasser, all behavior is made up of four components. If you want to increase your capacity for making new choices, it can help to first understand these components:

Dr. William Glasser's Four Components of Behavior

1. Acting: consists of active behaviors, such as walking, lifting, or even speaking, which all involve moving some part of your body.
2. Thinking: consists of those thoughts you generate both voluntarily and involuntarily, which both contribute to and proceed from your chosen actions.
3. Feeling: consists of the entire gamut of emotions that arise within you, from pleasurable to painful, which both contribute to and proceed from your chosen actions and thoughts.
4. Physiology: encompasses both the voluntary and involuntary body mechanisms involved in the acting, thinking, and feeling components of behavior.

All four behavior components are present all the time, but Glasser's approach asks us to name our current behavior at any moment by first considering the most obvious component. For example:

1. **Acting** – If I am onstage engaged in public speaking, the most obvious component of my behavior is the acting component. While I'm speaking, I'm also thinking. I might be thinking, "I wonder if they're enjoying my speech." While I'm speaking and thinking, I'm also certain to be feeling something. It might be exhilaration or fear. Simultaneously, my physiology gets in on the action: my heart rate might go up, or I might perspire. All four components comprise my total behavior, but the most obvious component is the action of "public speaking."
2. **Thinking** – Sometimes the thinking component of behavior takes the front seat—for example, when I'm analyzing a problem. While I'm analyzing, my acting behavior might be to jot down ideas on a notepad. My feeling component might be optimism or worry. My physiological state could be alert or sleepy. But it's clear that my thoughts are driving this behavior. So I name this behavior "analyzing a problem," based on its most obvious component: Thinking.

3. **Feeling** – One example of the feeling component of behavior is irritation. While I'm irritated, I might be thinking, "Why can't this person finish tasks on time?" I might be acting on completing the task myself. My physiology would likely include neck tension. But if I observe myself carefully in situations like this, I notice that the most prevalent sign of my behavior is the irritation, which would likely be the most observable component to anybody in the room.

4. **Physiological** – Wakefulness is one physiological component of behavior. While I'm wakeful, essentially very alive to the world around me, I might experience feelings of animated joy, accompanied by the thought, "Wow, life is great." All this might happen while I'm hiking on a nature trail, so an observer who doesn't know what's going on inside me might identify the action of hiking as my most obvious behavior component. Only I would know that I came out here primarily because I wanted to give free rein to the energy I'm feeling. My observing self recognizes my wakeful physiology as the most powerful engine driving this behavior.

We make choices every waking moment of our lives, so all four of the above components are collaborating all the time. Any time you make a new choice, one of the components changes, which causes the other three to shift with it. To empower yourself to make better choices, it can help to be aware of Glasser's four behavior components. Whether we face novel situations or familiar ones, our actions, thoughts, feelings, and physiological responses may offer us important clues about when we stand to benefit from a change in behavior.

How Brian Made a New Choice

Brian was a young up-and-comer in the petroleum industry who moved out of one functional area into another that was distinctly different. In my coaching sessions with Brian, he identified that his most problematic default settings involved fear of failure. He had a lot of trouble letting things go. One of the problems he was having was that he would bring his work home with him—not just his worries, his actual work. The moment he got home he would rush to the computer. "I get home and I'm not able to be there for my wife," he told me, "and I have a two-year-old and sometimes I barely get five minutes with him." This became a vicious cycle. It prevented him from making positive use of his family time to recharge, and prevented him from connecting with the sense of purpose his family gave him. When he showed up at work the next morning he would be just as stressed as he was when he left the night before. So it started all over again.

Brian decided that the biggest question he needed to consider to get back to choice was this: "What can I do at work so I'm not so worried about failure that I can't enjoy my time at home?"

Answering that question required him to observe his behavior throughout the day. We discovered that a lot of his stress came from difficult meetings in which he had to work with teams of engineers to address major systemic changes. Supervisors were angry about the changes and seemed to resist every directive or suggestion he gave them. He didn't know how to get them to stop resisting and start cooperating. Once we identified the problem, the next task was for him to consider making new choices during those meetings.

I suggested he try something similar to what Carla did, for different reasons. Unlike Carla, Brian is an extrovert, but asking questions can also offer a new way for an extrovert to experience a meeting. Here's what I told Brian: "What if you go into today's meeting and instead of trying to get people to do what you want, you just ask questions and listen so you can get into how they're thinking? Then maybe you can get a sense of why they're so antagonistic. Here's what I think will happen: first, I suspect it will shock the heck out of them because they're expecting the corporate hammer to come down; second, I think you'll leave with a better understanding of how to influence them. Do you want to test that hypothesis?"

He tried it, and when we spoke again he was excited to report three results: 1) He did surprise the heck out of them, so much so that they gave him feedback indicating they were grateful he was not like every other corporate bigwig who had come in trying to force something down their throats, 2) he learned a lot about their needs so he could tailor the changes to make the transition easier for them, and most importantly, 3) he wasn't tense, because he was simply listening and not struggling to figure out how to avoid failure.

That day, for the first time in weeks, he did not feel wound up when he got home. He kissed his wife, played with the baby, and relaxed without feeling an urgent need to run to his computer and solve an unsolvable issue. What's more, the issues no longer seemed unsolvable. In fact, Brian was talking about the fun of new challenges at work.

All because he made a choice to change a single action: from explaining to listening.

What We Can Control

The behavior component over which we have the most control is Acting. If we want to change our thoughts, feelings, or physiological state, we typically come up with the most efficient shift by changing our actions. However, that's not always possible. What if you face a situation where you can't change what you're doing? For example, you might be falling asleep in a meeting and your preferred action might be to leave and walk around the building. But maybe you cannot escape without signaling disengagement or irresponsibility. What then?

The next easiest behavioral component to change, after Acting, is Thinking. Pay attention to your thoughts. If you're thinking, "I'm bored," try asking yourself, "What aspect of this meeting does interest me?" Maybe a few minutes ago somebody proposed an idea that sparked your interest. Is there any connection between that idea and what's being discussed now? Can you think of a question to ask? Can you mentally plan what you'd like to contribute when your agenda item comes up later? Maybe you simply look around and notice that a few people look as listless as you feel, so you think of a different course of action: you suggest a five-minute break to refresh and regroup. Now your thoughts have led you back to action.

Although we always have choices, it's worth acknowledging that choices have limits. One controversy surrounding Glasser's Choice

Theory is that he considered everything in our lives a choice, even mental illness. As with any idea, regardless of its merits, it is possible to take Glasser's idea to extremes. I suggest treading cautiously with this one. You and I can surely think of situations in which bad things happen to good people regardless of behavior. Still, I agree with Glasser that, consciously or unconsciously, we're always making some sort of choice.

Even if we face a situation in which one aspect of our behavior seems outside our control—maybe feeling fear that we'll say the wrong thing at a meeting or noticing our heart racing every time we address an audience—typically at least one of our other behavioral components is still at our disposal. At the very least, we can consider a new action that might empower us: maybe learning to ask questions at a meeting, or meditating before giving a speech.

We don't always have all the choices we want in every situation, but we always have the option to notice the choices we do have. For example:

- Is this a good time to listen to someone else's idea or sell my own idea?
- Am I ready to discuss an uncomfortable subject that might lead to change, or is it more prudent keep this one close to the vest?
- Will it be more productive to face the conflict or avoid the conflict?
- Do I trust this person or not?

Those are all choices.

There are times to listen and times to sell. There are times when it is counterproductive to share information, and times when that's the best way to serve the needs of a project. There are times when confrontation can escalate a problem and times when it is the only way to clear the air and move forward. There are times to be cautious and times to trust.

You will never be able to judge all situations perfectly, but so long as you make choices with an awareness of your values and goals, your experience and knowledge, what has served you in the past and what you'd like to change about your future—then each choice will help you become a better chooser. Even when you make mistakes, that is part of the process of becoming an aware leader.

There is no way to move toward your values without making choices. When you make choices with self-awareness, you move toward your vision of who you want to be.

Every moment we face is the end of our past and the beginning of our future. To create a better future, we must accept the responsibility of making choices. That is how we put self-awareness to work. Right now is always the most powerful moment because it is the only moment in which we can choose a behavior. It is the only moment when an aware leader can make a decision that moves them toward their future.

A WORD TO THE AWARE LEADER:

*Destiny is no matter of chance. It is a matter of choice.
It is not a thing to be waited for, it is a thing to be achieved.*

—William Jennings Bryan

TEN

APPLY YOUR AWARENESS

Awareness Is Not Enough

Awareness is the first step to change, but awareness alone is not change. Intention is meaningless without action. If you want to become a better leader, it is not enough to simply become aware of who you are inside. You must then take action to become that person in your external life. Your thoughts and emotions, knowledge and experience, values and intuition become meaningless unless you act on them. If you don't act like the person you wish to be, then you will not become that person. This is what proponents of practical self-awareness call a need for "applied awareness."

Computer programmers often talk about "application awareness": a system's capacity to maintain information about a variety of interconnected applications. To optimize operational effectiveness, a computer system must monitor, diagnose, and interpret all of the applications it is juggling at any time, along with the information contained within those applications. In other words, a computer must be ready at all times to act on all the information in its system.

In many ways, a human being correlates to a complex computer system. To be effective at applied awareness, we must strive to be aware of what is happening in our minds and bodies at all times, and to be aware of all the information contained within that mind-body system.

That information includes external input from other people and our environment.

"You can give me all the awareness in the world, but you also have to be able to translate that into behavior. In Corporate America, it is okay to talk about behavior, but difficult to get beyond talking. That level is not deep enough to make an impact. It allows people to feel like they are changing when they really are not. It is very superficial." — Brian Sorge, Vice President of Client Affairs, Lambert & Associates33

What does applying our awareness mean in practical terms?

Authentically showing up the way you want to show up as a leader is not automatic. It is a voluntary act. Anyone who has made a resolution to stop smoking, start exercising, or stop or start any habit, knows how challenging it is to change behavior. Human beings are habit-bound. Behavioral scientist Norbert Schwarz explains that change is comprised of two processes that people deploy in stages. The first stage is developing awareness of a problem and the motivation to change that problem and experience relief.[34]

There is typically a gap between the first stage and the second stage, which Schwarz refers to as volition. Volition involves the actual planning and implementation of the behavioral change, which I refer to as choice. The second stage is challenging because it involves maintaining the new behavior over time.

Making the Choice to Change

Here is one method I have seen work for leaders who are ready to enact effective change:

- Choice 1: Write a story that describes the remarkable person you will be when you achieve your highest potential.
- Choice 2: Pick just one new choice you can make every day that will help carry you on a journey toward that potential.
- Choice 3: Each day make a decision to be remarkable, and with that decision commit to take every opportunity to make the new choice you have identified.

Because of the difficulty of maintaining a behavioral change over time, it is not enough to hope to change, try to change, or jump into the deep end and instantly change. What you need is an action plan, complete with goals, metrics for success, and rewards.

One of the greatest aids in maintaining new behaviors is to seek external support and accountability. According to psychologists Gregory M. Walton of Yale and Geoffrey L. Cohen of the University of Colorado, Boulder, our desire to experience belonging is a major motivator. If you want to change your behavior, seek people who model that behavior. They can become effective support systems and mirrors, motivating you to achieve the change you seek.

It's not necessary to overhaul your list of friends and colleagues to create a support system for change. With modern technology, we have more options than ever to find support. According to research published in 2011 in the journal *Translational Behavioral Medicine*, people seeking change in such areas as quitting smoking, losing weight, and managing medical treatment tend to see better results if they use personal digital assistants. PDAs provide individualized feedback, intervention strategies, and social support in pursuit of goals. I use an app called ACT Companion which sends me multiple messages a day to remind me to practice the skills of mindfulness: being present, opening up, and doing what matters.

As you grow into your role as an aware leader, you'll rely on fewer role models, because reaching your full potential calls on you to enhance that which makes you unique. Harvard Business School advises: "Break free. Start thinking and acting differently." Ultimately, you will come up with your own internal guidelines for best behavior.

If you wish to motivate yourself, it is critical that you understand why your values are important to you. Knowing your purpose can be a strong motivation. In self-motivation, you model your behavior after the future self you envision, checking in regularly not with peers or PDAs, but with the standard you set for yourself.

Bob Does Improv

Bob was a brilliant guy who was seen as the natural successor to become the next CEO of a multinational petroleum corporation, but the board had a few concerns about him. One concern was that Bob rarely spoke up in leadership meetings. He was an introvert who felt uncomfortable asserting himself in that environment. In many arenas, his focus on research, introspection, and making mental connections served him well. But it was not serving him in these meetings.

Bob was aware of that, but did not know how to change. That's where he turned to me as his coach. We explored his past, which helped with his awareness but did not lead to change. It was not as if knowing his past would turn him into an extrovert. Bob needed an action plan.

To achieve that, what was more critical than understanding his past was identifying when and how his introverted behavior showed up. Our next step was *not* to remove his introversion, but instead to find a new way to work with it, or around it. To help Bob decide on a plan of attack best suited to his personality, I asked if he'd ever had an experience in which he was comfortable speaking in front of a group.

He remembered, "I once made a presentation about petroleum chemistry to a large professional group at a conference. I felt confident then." He had worked in the oil business, and even though he was not a chemist, he had learned so much about the subject that he could hold his own with the scientists.

"Then the challenge here is not about public speaking," I said. "It seems to be about your great discomfort in extemporaneous situations."

"Right," Bob said. "I don't have security in doing that. I'm afraid I'm going to screw up."

"Do you remember what was different about that one experience that gave you the ability to be this relaxed guy, where in this other situation you were uncomfortable?"

"I knew my stuff. I was the expert."

"Can you be the expert in everything your new company does?"

"Probably not."

We talked about how he might reproduce the feeling of competency without being the expert, but we weren't getting anywhere. Then he let me throw an idea at him. "Why don't you take improv classes? Those are about being extemporaneous, about becoming an expert at that."

He decided to do it, but asked me to keep it a secret. The improv group he signed up to take classes with often does corporate work, but it was important to him to maintain privacy. He chose to forgo the corporate classes and instead took the same classes that aspiring comedians take.

The workshop took three months. The graduation ceremony featured a Sunday-night performance by the entire comedy troupe, including Bob. He was excited to report to me that it was a hit. The course taught him a new way to be present and listen, an important part of being able to respond. One empowering perspective he learned was that "there is no wrong response." It was all about listening in a different way so that you're not stuck in your head.

He brought that spirit to meetings with fellow leaders and discovered a new ability to be more present and vocal with colleagues. He developed a different type of competency to help him feel secure in those meetings. He discovered he did not have to be an expert on the subject at hand. He instead became an expert at being fully present and participating.

Bob's peers soon saw him as worthy of leading. He is now president of the corporation.

Notice that Bob's awareness itself did not provide the impetus to change. He needed to make a plan, and he enlisted help in implementing his plan—in his case, the help of an executive coach *and* improv instructors. His plan included a goal: completing a three-month improv workshop. The class had metrics: he had to show up weekly, learn to listen differently, and perform at a graduation. He received the reward of learning he did not need to have all the right answers in order to be good at extemporaneous speaking. He also received the reward of laughter, applause, and praise from his audience and his fellow performers when he spoke up.

The skills Bob learned in improv translated into practical leadership techniques he could put into action at meetings: listening instead of planning what to say, asking questions rather than pressuring himself to know all the answers, not judging his comments based on whether they were right or wrong but on whether they contributed to the process.

Bob made a new habit that will likely last him a lifetime. He did so by applying his self-awareness to learning a new skill and developing an ongoing course of action that works for him.

Mindfulness Takes Practice

Awareness is a little like succeeding at a new diet. You cannot merely "go on a diet" until you reach your goal weight and then go back to eating the way you used to. If you do, you'll gain all the weight back. The key is to decide to make a lifetime change in the way you eat. The goal is not only to reach a specific weight, but also to make a set of healthy new habits that you will engage in for the rest of your life. Similarly, once you become aware of your challenges as a leader and create strategies to deal with them, you cannot merely use those new strategies until you achieve the position you want and then go back to your old ways.

What's more, you cannot rely on your new strategies to kick in on their own. Stress is very good at bringing out the juvenile in us, the person we were before we developed our new habits. You'll need to stay vigilant to prevent that. That means you'll need to maintain active awareness of what's going on with you for the rest of your life, and you'll need to be ready to put your strategies into action whenever you feel one of your derailing behaviors coming on.

One strategy to help you maintain new habits is to engage your observing self to stay on top of your thoughts, emotions, and somatics. Somatics refers to the way your body reacts to changes throughout the day. All of this takes practice. You will never be done practicing.

Please don't confuse the need for awareness with vigilance, which can be counterproductive. Awareness does not mean knowing everything. Rather, it's a matter of paying attention to your attention. If you disappear into your head for a moment, no need to panic. As an aware leader, you now know how to tell yourself, "Good for you for noticing that you vanished. Now just come on back to the moment. Welcome back!"

Practicing advanced awareness, like listening to your intuition, will never be a perfect process. You can listen to everything your mind and body have to say and accept it all as information worth processing. That does not mean you'll reach a point when you always make the right decisions. However, the more information you open yourself to, the more choices you have, and the more choices you have, the more effective your leadership becomes.

Two simple things I do—and advise all my clients to do—to maintain self-awareness like a well-oiled machine, is to check in with myself in the morning and again at night.

I suggest you prime the pump of self-awareness every morning by pausing to contemplate the opportunities and challenges you foresee in the day ahead. This mental process can take as little as a minute or as long as an hour, depending on your needs. Some do it while lying in bed, standing in the shower, sitting in meditation, or listening to music in the car, whatever it takes to get your mind quiet so you can connect with yourself. All you need to ask is, "What does life have to offer me today?" Maybe you'll respond with a mental list, focus on one big possibility, or just consider the first opportunity of the day. It's all up to your unique style.

How can I allow my soul to reach its full potential today?

As an aware leader, you already know it's not enough to look ahead toward possibility, it's also important to look back and measure achievement. So, checking in with yourself at the beginning of the day is only half the process. It's equally important to check in with yourself at day's end and reflect on all the opportunities that came up—without judgment. I'll admit it's not easy, even for self-assured leaders. "Damn, I missed that moment!" I hear it all the time. But that's good information for tomorrow. Just make sure you don't only focus on the moments you missed, but also recognize the moments you grabbed hold of and made work.

When my clients create a new habit, at first they always notice how often they blow it. That's because they're working on awareness. I always ask, "Think of one time today when you did make the choice you wanted to make. What does it tell you? That you can do it! If you did it once, you can do it again."

Even if you take advantage of one opportunity a day, that's a strong foundation for aware leadership.

Frank Hits Pause

When things are stressful, it's not enough to check in only at the start and finish of the day. If you face especially big challenges, it's important to take opportunities to pause in the middle of the day and check in with yourself again. Pausing is a great way to get to know yourself in the moment, by getting in tune with your senses, your intuition, and your memory.

In stressful situations, it can help to ask yourself, "What am I remembering?" Default settings come from memories. When we know what we're remembering, sometimes that can prevent us from derailing and keep us present. What's more, memories can also lead to solutions, especially if they're memories of similar situations in which you made a choice that worked. When you're ready to take that a step further, try asking yourself, "What am I intuiting?" That is really powerful, to be so in tune with mind and body in the moment that you trust yourself to make an intuitive leap. That is applying awareness with gusto!

A lot of applied awareness is simply a matter of getting back into your five senses. Pause and ask yourself: what am I feeling, seeing, hearing, smelling, tasting?

One of my clients is the CEO of a technology company in the Northwest. In recent years, technology professionals found themselves dealing with major changes that created a lot of stress. In Frank's city, a small tech company went up for sale just down the street from one of his offices. He pushed for his company to buy it, based partly on the hope that it would give them access to new customers. The board decided not to go for it, which created a stressful new situation for Frank.

The state where Frank worked had a limited pool of technology talent, and now a new health organization was coming on board to compete for their attention. All this was happening amid industry-wide speculation about what the many new changes in America's technology industry would bring. Some employees believed the changes would reduce their earnings, while others believed the changes represented an opportunity to increase their earnings if they could find the right leverage. Frank worried that many employees would jump ship to try to position themselves to survive the storm and come out stronger on the other side.

Frank's system ran a top technology think tank, and he was concerned about the risk of losing his best engineers to the competition. He told me he felt discouraged by the attitudes of some of the intellectual talent who reported to him: "It feels like some of them have lost sight of their mission. I want to tell them, 'You're here for to impact the future, not for yourself.'" His greatest fear was that if he lost the hospital's cardiac facility he might lose his job.

Frank's concerns were legitimate. Technology was moving at an accelerated rate, and as a result heads have rolled. But while Frank did need to be aware of the reality of his situation, he also needed to be aware that he could not control the future.

There is a big difference between acknowledging real concerns and catastrophizing those concerns.

One reality check Frank needed to remember was that the board chose him for his visionary ability to see a way through problems where others could not. Sometimes he was afraid of their belief in him because of the chance that he might fail expectations. But if anyone could solve the potential brain drain from his technology company, he could—so long as he kept his head in the game and did not catastrophize.

When Frank catastrophized, he was no longer in the moment. He was playing a tape in his head of the worst things that could happen if he didn't solve his organization's problems. He needed to separate the real problems he had the power to address from the imagined catastrophe that might result from things he could not control. For example, yes he might lose his job, but no, his family would not end up on the street.

To put a stop to the spiral of catastrophizing, Frank has learned to pause. These days, when he needs to, he literally stops for a moment: stops talking, stops doing, stops deciding, and shifts to his observing self. His observing self asks, "What's going on with me physically, mentally, and emotionally? Do I feel stuck in a default setting? Am I spiraling around thoughts like, 'My father always said I couldn't do anything right!' Or am I present to what's going on? What choice can I make right now that would take me out of panic and return me to neutral?"

Pausing can be like meditation, tuning in to the present moment while detaching from your thoughts and feelings about that moment.

You're not *doing* anything. You're just being. This allows you to realign with who you are: What is the information? What are my values? What is my default setting? What are my objectives? What are my choices?

Sometimes Frank simply notices that his chest feels tight and he's not breathing deeply, so he takes a minute to do the breathing exercise from Mindful Moment #1. This helps him disconnect from negative spirals. Then he's ready to make choices again, not from a place of panic, but from a place of being in the moment and identifying what's real.

One day Frank called me to share a breakthrough in his self-awareness. He had just taken a flight to Chicago for a critical negotiation and his mind was racing, so he took out his iPad to read. The book that popped up was one I had recommended, *The Happiness Trap* by Russ Harris. He read a chapter that helped him realize he was engaged in boxed-in thought patterns: repeating conversations from relationships gone sour, lamenting lost opportunities and perceived injustices, and gnawing on future aches and pains, all of which robbed him of peace of mind. He named this thought pattern the *Self-recrimination Box*. More importantly, he accepted it. He told me that this made him feel free. I could sense his relief through my cell phone.

That day he moved forward in his thinking. He decided to take action every day to lessen the impact of his Self-recrimination Box. His plan included bookending each day with moments for reflection, as well as taking planned pauses throughout the day. He didn't start ignoring the thoughts and feelings that once threatened to derail him, but now he found it easier to hold them loosely, face them, and move on. With that, he developed greater emotional agility, which allowed him to respond more compassionately, to both himself and others, Frank did less catastrophizing. Once he felt less panicked about losing physicians, he was free to find new ways to communicate with them.

Frank did lose a few doctors to the competition, but most stayed, and several replacements came on board who shared his value of patient care as a top priority. His think tank is still internationally renowned, and Frank is still in charge, navigating his organization's way into the future.

Moving to a More Mindful You

Being a detached self-observer while also taking action can feel like playing two roles. There's no question it is challenging. If it weren't, everybody would choose to be a leader.

All of us, from laborers to CEOs, need the help of tools to do our jobs. I find the Mindful Moments exercises throughout this book are useful as tools that help pry leaders loose from old patterns of behavior, indecisiveness, and the temptation to cling to the familiar instead of embracing change. Here's one I find useful for people who have trouble making the leap from awareness to action:

MINDFUL MOMENT #6:
OBSERVING THE MOMENT

Objective: to become more aware of your emotions, thoughts, sensations, and triggers during a conversation with a supervisor or colleague.

Instructions: Prior to your next conversation with the person in question, practice aware breathing (see Mindful Moment #1) to gain presence. After the conversation, find a space by yourself, pull out a pad and pen, and invite your observing self to answer the following:

1. What am I feeling?
2. What are my thoughts? What is my inner dialogue?
3. How did I show up to this conversation? What was my mood?
4. What judgments and assessments do I have about this person?
5. What judgments and assessments do I have about this conversation?
6. What were the outcomes of our conversation?

Remember, your observing self is detached. Observe the conversation without judgment, write down your answers, and then take a few moments to reflect on your observations.

Incorporating the observing self into your daily way of being is critical. Until you become mindful of what's going on inside you, you cannot effectively turn self-awareness into action.

Sometimes the Right Thing to Do Is Nothing

Putting awareness into action does not mean you always need to take action. Life is not a superhero movie in which catastrophe strikes every few minutes and the hero must always save the day. One of the ways leaders put awareness into action is by choosing to step back.

Leaders sometimes confuse being a leader with doing things that look like leadership. If you ever feel a lack of control and are tempted to say, "I don't understand why I feel out of control, look at all I'm doing!" that's a good moment to pause and ask, "Do I really need to be doing so much or am I just trying to make sure everyone knows I'm in control?" Leaders with strong self-awareness are less interested in *doing* leadership than they are in *being* leaders.

"Think of your conventional sense of self. Is this a real conception of self, or is it confused with complex activities, or with concepts and impressions about who you think you are?"

— Lolly Daskal, Lead From Within blog

When you know who you are and what you value, and make choices based on that, you are on the path to becoming a great human being. On the other hand, when you go through a series of motions that look important without knowing why you are doing them, you risk becoming a *human doing*.

Being and doing each depend on the other for fulfillment. On one hand, being a great leader on the inside without doing anything to reveal those qualities is meaningless. On the other hand, if your actions are not fueled by who you are within, then your actions also become meaningless. When you're unsure of whether or not to take action, here's a good question to ask yourself: "Am I equally as interested in who I'm being as in what I'm doing?"

Expand Your Mind

If we want to take our leadership as far as it can go, then applied awareness must mean more than simply subtracting bad habits and adding good ones. If we want to grow into our full potential, then we will create opportunities to diversify our experiences. Seeking new experiences is another way to push our awareness forward to develop new behaviors, styles, and preferences. I'm not simply talking about seeking new experiences as a strategy to overcome derailing behavior, like Bob did when he took the improv class to overcome his fear of extemporaneous speaking. I'm talking about something more.

When you seek new experiences you create opportunities: to discover a side of yourself you never knew existed or create a new aspect of yourself that never existed before.

I grew up in a lower middle class family, and when I received a scholarship to attend Baylor University I took advantage of the opportunity to expose myself to new experiences. My scholarship did not pay for everything, so I worked my way through college washing dishes in my dorm's cafeteria. I was one of the few white employees among many African Americans. Two of them, Ed and Eunice, took me under their wings. I had grown up in a segregated part of East Texas. There was not a single African American in my hometown, so this friendship alone was a new experience. The opportunity did not end there.

One day, Ed and Eunice told me that the famed blues guitarist and singer Freddie King was coming to play at a black nightclub across the river from our college. It was literally on the other side of the water from where most of the white people lived.

I said, "Freddie King? Wow, I'd love to hear him perform live! He's incredible."

"Go with us," Ed said. "It's a big dance. There'll be about two thousand people there."

I jumped at the chance. I wasn't thinking about the event being black or white. I just wanted to hear one of my favorite musicians play.

Eunice was thinking ahead, though, and she asked, "Do you know how to dance?"

I laughed. "You've gotta be joking. I'm a big klutz. I can't dance."

During our breaks at the cafeteria, Eunice took it upon herself to take me out on the dock and try to teach me to dance. It wasn't long before we were both laughing at my hopeless awkwardness. There was just no connection between my brain and my legs. Eunice finally gave up. "You're right. You can't dance."

I still went to the concert. I was surprised to discover that I was the only white person in sight among two thousand people. It was the first time I had ever been in a place where I was not in the majority. I did receive a few skeptical looks, and if it hadn't been for Ed and Eunice I might have felt insecure. Either way, it was a great experience. Freddie King was an incredible performer, and the enthusiastic crowd was fun to watch and be a part of.

A couple of years later, I returned to Baylor as a pastor and took the opportunity to preach at a black church. It was an extraordinary experience, because the church was different from white churches I was used to. Everyone felt involved in the service on every level. I might not have had the courage to do it if Ed and Eunice had not taken me to the Freddie King concert.

Those early steps outside my comfort zone ultimately made it easier for me to feel comfortable with working internationally in human resources, which I did for many years, logging two million miles of travel around the world. I had never even set foot on a plane until I got out of college. I didn't even have a passport until I was forty-two years old.

Each time I stepped out of my comfort zone, and not only survived but thrived, helped me to envision myself taking the next step and then, most importantly, to take it.

If you want to find out what strong leadership material you're made of, stretch beyond the limits to which you're accustomed. Go to places you've only dreamed, do things you never dreamed, and reach out to people who weren't even on your radar. Awareness will never take your leadership as far as it can go unless you take action. You need to not only wake up to who you are, but also to take the aware new you out for a spin and see what that baby can do!

A WORD TO THE AWARE LEADER:

"Watch your thoughts, they become words.
Watch your words, they become actions. Watch your actions,
they become habits. Watch your habits, they become character.
Watch your character, it becomes your destiny."

—Anonymous

ELEVEN

MAKE YOUR OUTSIDE
MATCH YOUR INSIDE

Do We See Ourselves as We Really Are?

How accurate is your self-image? Are you aware of how you show up in the world as a spouse, parent, friend, son, daughter, neighbor, colleague, or leader? Experience has shown me that to be aware leaders, we must regularly seek ways to reconcile two different selves: the external self and the internal self.

The external self is at home in the physical, social, and interactive functions of daily life. It works constantly to make things happen, to accomplish goals, relate to others, and handle changing situations. The external self has expectations, rules, and procedures, all set up to protect us in the face of the world's complex demands. The mantra of the external self is "reason and willpower." As long as reason and willpower don't break down, we get things done.

Enter the internal self, which operates in the world of impressions formed throughout our lives. It has a strong viewpoint about what the external world is like, what to watch out for, and what we can trust. Even among those of us with a strong self-image, the internal self's strong attachment to history can predispose us to ignore rational information and dismiss feedback.

The quality of your external life greatly depends on the quality of your internal life. Your characteristic thoughts and the content of your subconscious determine the way you act and react. A high-quality emotional and mental life allows you to know when characteristic thoughts and your subconscious are serving you, and when they are not. When you learn to observe the way you feel and think about things, and the way you react to people and situations, you have the power to choose new actions and behaviors.

When the inner self is aware, it positively influences the external self.

People talk about their perceptions of the external world all the time: "I heard on the radio that bureaucrat resigned because of that scandal," or "You should buy a computer from this company because they have the best service," or "I suggest taking a coat because it's cold out." Humans are predisposed to catalog our external experience. But if you think about it, the way you see things on the outside is based on how you feel and think on the inside. For example, if somebody who had never seen a city saw one for the first time, that person would have no frame of reference for it, so they would likely experience it very differently from someone who had spent a lifetime in a city.

Everything we see is colored by emotion, opinion, and memory. Although we think we see things as they are, it is truer to say that we see things as *we* are. It's important to be aware of that because it impacts the way we interact with people. People who are not self-aware can find it difficult to understand how their internal self affects their external experience, and therefore their way of interacting with the world. The more we look inward for understanding, the better we become at differentiating what's going on within ourselves from what's going on out there.

Does Your Personality Reflect You?

Considering your own personality can be a little like looking at yourself in a mirror. Although you do see some things about yourself, you never get a complete picture of the way the world sees you. Meanwhile, you might know something about what's going on inside you, but others only infer what you hold within you from what they see you doing on the outside.

When we consider the impressions we make on others and the perspectives others hold about us, we call that reputation. According to the *Five-Factor Model of Personality* by psychologist Jerry S. Wiggins, reputation can be measured in terms of five dimensions.

FIVE DIMENSIONS OF PERSONALITY – JERRY S. WIGGINS35

- Nervous and moody to calm and assured
- Quiet and unassertive to active and outgoing
- Impulsive and careless to conscientious and conforming
- Hard-nosed and tough to tactful and sensitive
- Narrow and unimaginative to curious and imaginative

Becoming self-aware is not only about knowing who you are, but also knowing who other people believe you are. If you want to understand yourself, you need to understand both your personal identity and your reputation. Reputation *describes* your behavior, while identity *explains* it. There is, in everyone, a gap between reputation and identity, between the way we see ourselves and the way others see us. Part of this is because nobody else will ever know us fully, but part of it may also be because we do not see ourselves fully. There is usually a gap between who we want to be and who we really are. We need not let that worry us. That is where the work of self-awareness comes in to help us grow, which is a lifelong journey.

In between the passive stage of recognizing the need for change and the active process of implementing change, which we looked at in Chapter Ten, there is a complex transition that happens. During that transition, we find ourselves taking a harder look at the way we are on the inside and the way we want to become on the outside. In other words, we take a look at who we want to be and who our reputation says we are.

To Gain Awareness of Your Reputation:

- Observe how you get along with others.
- Observe how you get ahead or achieve status.
- Observe yourself from two perspectives: yours and that of others who observe you.

We all use internal skills to develop strategies for pursuing external acceptance and status. Those strategies form a basis for the way we see ourselves, which is our *identity*. Meanwhile, our efforts to implement those strategies to get along or get ahead reveal themselves in episodic behaviors. Those behaviors form the basis for the way others see us, which is our *reputation*. There are substantial differences in the way we understand our efforts to get along or get ahead versus the way others evaluate those efforts.

Getting along with others takes cooperation, friendliness, and a positive attitude. We know we're getting along when people seek our advice, invite us to work with them, or call us "team players." Getting ahead requires seeking responsibility, competing to be recognized, and motivating others. We know we're getting ahead when we achieve results, motivate those who work for us achieve results, and rise to higher levels of authority. All those things form the basis for a reputation as a genuine leader. Better self-knowledge can help us achieve that reputation.

It's important to recognize that having a reputation for leadership is not merely about people recognizing your capacity for success. It's also about people recognizing the strength of character you bring to both smooth sailing and rough seas, to both your achievements and your setbacks. Talent does not equal perfection. Even if you have the knowledge, experience, and skills to perform a leadership role, all humans face limitations under stress. To grow as a leader, you must understand those limitations.

Leaders who don't practice self-awareness often have distorted beliefs about themselves, about how others react to them, and about the best means to achieve their goals. That sort of disconnect between identity and reputation can have devastating consequences. I'm not only referring to leaders who engage in high-profile negative behaviors like dishonesty, violence, or indiscretion. I'm saying the subtle behaviors that pervade your day-to-day interactions, the kinds of things you're most likely to overlook in yourself, have the power to hurt your reputation.

It's risky to assume you'll never be at risk for providing poor leadership just because you have the knowledge, experience, and skills your position requires. At the executive level, people's perceptions of you become the reality of your leadership. It's not enough to understand the job. You also need to understand yourself and the way you show up in the world.

If you seek enduring satisfaction in your life and career, seek a deep understanding of your values and interests, and seek to act in concert with those things. This is the beginning of creating a reputation in which your thoughts, words, and actions are consistent. This is the beginning of people recognizing your leadership, by recognizing that first and foremost, you are who you say you are. This is the beginning of making the external you match the internal you, so that the world sees you as you want to be.

Reputation is a fluid thing. I identify myself as an outgoing guy and raconteur with a tendency to dominate conversations. Sometimes this gives me a reputation for being lively, interesting, and commanding. Other times it can give me a reputation for coming on too strong, being self-absorbed, and showing little interest in others. This need not turn into derailing behavior, so long as I strive to be aware of the internal mechanisms that cause me to behave the way I do, and to be aware of the perceptions my behaviors elicit in others.

At first, leaders may fear to find out the way others see them. Then, once they do find out, they may be mortified at how little it matches the way they want to be seen. In the end, we find that seeing ourselves as we are is both humbling and freeing, which isn't so bad. Being aware of the way people perceive us gives us an opportunity to make more informed choices about how to interact with others for optimal impact.

The problem with trying to gauge your reputation is that your observations of yourself are bound to be incomplete. If I think people see me as a charming storyteller, then every time people laugh at my jokes or listen to me with rapt attention I might let that validate my perception. I might fail to notice that I'm not giving them opportunities to interject. I might not consider the possibility that someone can find me funny while still feeling unhappy that I'm controlling the conversation. If I never ask anyone what's really going on in those situations, I run the risk of developing a point of view about my reputation with no data to support it.

I recently experienced this sort of disconnect from the other side of the conversation. I was on the phone with a woman who seemed to lack awareness of how she was coming across.

At one point she made a request, and I said, "Okay, I'll get that to you tomorrow."

Not five minutes later, she said, pressing harder, "This is really important, I really need you to..." and repeated her request.

I wanted to say, "I've already said yes," but I didn't know her well enough and didn't want to risk offending her.

Perhaps that woman had a fear of people not keeping their word or worried that people never listened to her. I didn't know. What I did know, and what she probably didn't, was that her habit of repeating herself came across as quirky. I wasn't in a position to give her feedback, so I didn't, but it was clear that she could have used feedback from someone.

Here's the importance of seeking external sources to validate, or invalidate, our self-perceptions: it gives us the opportunity to learn how to leverage our behavior to help us engage in more successful interactions. I've learned that I'm not always perceived as the delightful raconteur I think I am. That's okay. Some days I can have fun with that side of myself, but now I know that at other times I need to rein it in and call on my other personality traits to get results.

Feedback Anemia

Your identity is your internal view of who you are, while reputation is an external view of who you are. Since we don't always have an accurate understanding of the external view of who we are, I suggest assessments such as the Hogan Personality Inventory to help fill in gaps in our understanding. Hogan looks at seven attributes that measure a person's reputation.

SEVEN ATTRIBUTES OF REPUTATION
(FROM THE HOGAN PERSONALITY INVENTORY)

1. Adjustment: how you deal with stress, self-acceptance, range of emotional expression
2. Ambition: the drive to achieve, to lead, to socially interact
3. Social Ability: introversion versus extroversion
4. Interpersonal sensitivity: your reputation for empathy, sensitivity, trust, friendliness
5. Prudence: Are you an orderly person who follows rules, or a maverick who believes rules are made to be broken?
6. Inquisitive: Where do you fall on the spectrum from highly practical and conservative to highly innovative and creative?
7. Learning Orientation: Are you highly motivated to learn before doing, or do you prefer to just dive into the mix and figure it out?

Answering the above questions on your own is helpful, as it can give you some clues about how others see you, much like a mirror. However, like a mirror, it is not a complete picture. Sometimes we strive to be a certain way and assume that therefore we are that way. While you can identify much of the above information about yourself, the question will remain: how accurate is your understanding of the way others perceive the above traits in you?

Feedback can provide insightful information about your reputation, rounding out your self-awareness. Some great tools for feedback include psychometric assessments, performance reviews, and 360-feedback—collecting information about you not only from yourself, but also from others who work with you. Unfortunately, such assessments typically only happen once a year or less, and I've found that leaders are most effective when they receive feedback more often than that.

It is possible to regularly receive useful feedback about yourself from others, if you are truly open to the results. To elicit effective 360-feedback, you only need to focus on two main questions:

1. When I'm at my best as a leader, what am I doing?
2. To be even more effective, what could I do?

I would first ask those questions of yourself. Then I would ask them of your employees, colleagues, or those to whom you report. Don't be surprised if you find out that you see yourself more positively than others see you. Most leaders do. Even leaders who are aware they have low self-esteem sometimes underestimate the impact it has on others. At first, it can be disappointing to find out that we don't shine as brightly for others as we hoped. But let's face it, most people don't see even the greatest leaders as the center of the universe. This is a humbling opportunity for a reality check. It's your opportunity to enhance the external view you have of yourself, to step inside the mirror and get a good look around. If self-awareness is the key to effective leadership, then 360-degree self-awareness is the golden ticket.

Few executives have a complex understanding of the way others perceive them. That information can give you an edge.

If 360-feedback is so important, and if most leaders know about 360-feedback, then why do today's leaders so often suffer from what I call feedback anemia?

I believe the answer lies in the old adage: *It's lonely at the top.* Once leaders reach top executive levels, most of their colleagues are subordinates. They receive infrequent mentoring, coaching, and monitoring of their progress aside from the occasional performance review from a board of directors or senior supervisor, and those people rarely see the leader in action. For many executives, the air at the top is rarefied. They become isolated from regular feedback. The very people they are leading, the people who will respond to them and carry out their plans, often feel too intimidated to be candid. Who wants to criticize the boss? Or to look obsequious by heaping on praise? Meanwhile, the executive might not see it as wise to reveal concerns about his or her performance, to those above or below, for fear of appearing weak.

So, executives are less likely to receive feedback than most people in an organization. Yet, as leaders responsible for guiding and directing an organization, they often need feedback more than anyone. If you're an executive, how can you receive reliable feedback? The answer is: by never allowing yourself to become isolated from constructive criticism or strategic advice. Unfortunately, my experience in working with senior executives is that this is the very thing that usually happens. After years of getting feedback, its sudden absence can be seductive, leaving the executive with a sense that he or she is doing everything well. That can be hard to give up.

Beware being seduced by the absence of criticism. That flattering silence is lying to you! You did not become infallible just because you were put in charge, and deep down you know it. To become an aware leader, you need to know where your choices are working and where they aren't. Making those around you feel secure in giving you feedback is essential to your wellbeing as a leader, and to the wellbeing of your organization.

How often should you request feedback?

I've observed that requesting feedback monthly is too often. It can overwhelm the people from whom you request it. Around once a quarter is a good target, picking three to five touch-points over the course of the year. Don't ask the same person for feedback every time, either. You'll receive more complete information if you have a stable of people you listen to: junior, equal, and senior to you.

It's dangerous to accept a status quo that assumes the leader can do no wrong. Integrating self-perception with feedback from others is an important step to a leader's awareness.

If you feel hesitant about asking for frequent feedback, you're not alone. People tend to avoid feedback because they associate it with negative or corrective information. That's not the point. You are not seeking to learn something so simplistic as whether you're doing a "good job" or a "bad job." Rather, you are only seeking where your choices serve you and where they don't. You are not seeking shame or praise, but information that puts you at greater choice.

Interestingly, I've found that leaders who recognize the need for feedback are rarely defensive or averse to criticism. However they often cite lack of time. I strive to impress upon such people that feedback is not an extra that can be thrown overboard to cut time wastage, but rather an integral tool of management. In fact, because feedback builds trust, communication, and fluid problem solving, it ultimately saves time.

Here are a few straightforward steps you can take to invite responses to how you're doing in any given circumstance:

INVITING CANDID, CONSTRUCTIVE FEEDBACK

- Recognize that no manager, not even the CEO, can improve or maintain performance without feedback.
- Know that employees rarely volunteer feedback to managers, especially senior executives. Most believe that criticizing someone in power could backfire.
- Embrace feedback questions that promote a sense of contributing helpful information rather than criticism, and that

reduce a sense of fear or defensiveness, both for you and the person providing feedback:
  - When I'm at my best as a leader, what am I doing?
  - To be even more effective, what could I do?
- Establish trust every time you solicit feedback:
  - Accept the feedback without retort or defense.
  - Take time to reflect on the feedback, keeping in mind that deciding which feedback to act on and which to let go is your choice.
  - If you hear the same, or similar, feedback from multiple sources, pay attention.
  - Say "Thank You."
- When appropriate and genuine, close the loop on feedback you have received, sharing the ways in which it was helpful.

As we get to know ourselves better, feedback becomes a less challenging process. We learn how to put the information we receive into perspective, and how to allow it to help us achieve our dreams.

Even though senior executives typically have the portfolio required for their job, this does not preclude the need to continue experiential learning, hone skills, and increase knowledge. An extreme example I will never forget is when I recommended a book to a COO, who happened to be my supervisor at the time. He responded, "I don't read books. I know what I need to know to run this business." Let me tell you, his direct reports all thought he needed to read that book. But he never sought feedback, so he did not know that his perception of himself as someone on top of it all did not match his reputation.

Before they embark on any initiative, smart executives seek out information about all their projects, capital, action plans, and opportunities. They need to have this same discipline with their identity and their reputation. It's critical that senior executives gather information about their behavior from multiple sources. Recognizing the connection between your external and internal leader is an important step in establishing an organization that performs effectively from the top down.

A WORD TO THE AWARE LEADER:

"The way to gain a good reputation is to endeavor to be what you desire to appear."

—Socrates

 BIG CHANGES START WITH SMALL STEPS

Your Subconscious Will Resist Change

If this book has opened you to a new awareness of yourself, and if you are ready to put that knowledge into action, congratulations on embracing your power to make new choices as an aware leader. However, I'm going to tell you something counterintuitive: if you want to make big changes, slow down. You might be prepared to deal with resistance from others, but few are ever fully prepared for the inevitable resistance from their own subconscious.

Subconscious resistance to change is called *reversal*. We often hold on to negative emotions, counterproductive beliefs, and hurtful memories because we receive payoffs of which we're unaware. For example, a person who has suffered tragic loss in the past might find that, although lingering on depressing thoughts can be unproductive, it also invites attention, sympathy, and tolerance. It might be difficult to let that go of that, especially if change seems to require working harder for less recognition. Whatever you seek to change, remember you've had your habits for a long time and may be more comfortable with them than you realize.

Resistance to change is not just a refuge of the stubborn, foolish, or weak. It is the result of a useful human adaptation. The subconscious is good at developing survival strategies. Once it figures out what works, it resists changing its methods, even when a method is no longer useful. So, although you find the thought of moving in a new direction exciting, your subconscious will most likely do its utmost to keep you rooted right where you are. This place, these people, this routine all feel safe and familiar.

"Don't kick down the door of opportunity. Nor should you lock it. Just take small steps to it, slowly turn the handle, pull it open gently, and take a step inside." – Amber Hope

So here you are, eager to move forward, and you don't want your subconscious to throw your gears into reverse. What can you do? Pay attention to your thoughts. When your subconscious tries to sabotage your new choices, your thoughts will exhibit early warning signs. I assure you the following thoughts are perfectly normal, but although they sound convincing, the only reason you want to pay attention to them is so you can plan strategies to counteract their potential power to derail you:

ARGUMENTS YOUR SUBCONSCIOUS MIGHT USE TO STOP YOU FROM CHANGING:

- I don't deserve to make this change.
- It's not possible to make this change.
- It's not safe to make this change.
- I'll lose my identity if I make this change.
- I don't want to let go of my routine because I'm comfortable with it.
- This habit has always helped me maintain control over my behavior and keep my life in working order. How will I do that if I change?

- I don't want to let go of my old ways, because people will stop giving me the attention, understanding, and help I need.

How do you deal with the voice in your head when it gives you the above warnings? Tell it you don't plan to change all at once. The secret to lasting change is to take small steps.

One Small Step

Every journey begins with a single step, including the journey to a more aware you. Taking small steps is the key to convincing your subconscious to accept change. When you make incremental but intentional adjustments, your internal gatekeeper is less likely to sabotage you. Small changes don't feel as dangerous to the equilibrium your subconscious wants. You might be frustrated with the slow pace, but you'll feel less stressed and more satisfied with the results. My experience working with successful executives has revealed five reasons for that:

WHY SMALL STEPS LEAD TO MORE EFFECTIVE CHANGE

1. Low threshold: Taking small steps requires less energy, motivation, and trust. This makes it less likely you'll be thrown off track by such excuses as being too busy, having more important priorities, or being uncertain of the outcome.

2. Low risk: Great leaps may achieve a lot at once, but they require great precision. Robbie Knievel's jump over the Grand Canyon in 1999 was astonishing. The risk to life and limb was equally astonishing. Small steps have the advantage of not requiring a high degree of certainty to be effective. If the step does not work, not much will be lost. The chance of damage and wasted energy is minimal. You can easily return to the status quo if need be. Small steps

allow you to maintain flexibility. Given life's unpredictability, this is a huge advantage.

3. Positive message: If you try to make a huge change, your subconscious might take that to imply you have been doing everything wrong until now. Aiming for a small step implies that there is a lot functioning well as it is. If you build on success, rather than trying to come back from failure, you are more likely to feel motivated to follow through.

4. Positive ripple effects: The "one small step" approach has a side benefit: it can lead to a ripple effect. In their book Facilitating Organizational Change: Lessons from Complexity Science, authors Edwin Olson and Glenda Eoyang describe this ripple effect as follows: "A small change in one part ripples through the organization and can have tremendous unintended consequences far from the site of the intervention."36 Small changes in your behavior can have positive effects on your leadership, which positively affects those you come in contact with, which affects those they come in contact with, and so on.

5. Cumulative effects: Did you know that if you read just twenty minutes a day you can finish reading thirty-seven books a year? Take one step a day toward your vision of yourself and sooner or later you will get there. Even if you do just one new thing every week, you can make tremendous progress. Read one article, practice one new skill, make one new connection, eliminate one piece of clutter, or complete one more task in your big plan, and by the end of the year you'll be fifty-two steps closer to where you want to be.

Now that you know why taking one small step can be the most effective way to change, try this next exercise to determine what your optimal first step might be:

Choose Your First Step

1. Think about one change you want to make in your behavior that will take you one step closer to being the leader you want to be or achieving the results you want to achieve.

2. Now, on a scale of zero to ten, rate the way that behavior currently shows up in your life, with zero representing that aspect of your behavior at its worst and ten representing that aspect of your behavior at its best. This is not precise math; just go with your gut.

3. Let's say you score your current behavior at five. How long will it take you to get to ten? Here's what I'm betting: getting to a ten is too big a goal for this week or even next.

4. So, what small step would you need to take to get you to a six? Write down that step.

5. What are just a few external and internal signs that will tell you when you move one point up the scale? Write those down too.

6. How long will it take for you to climb that one point up the scale?

If your answer to question 6 is between a day and a few weeks, you are now looking at a perfect first step for you.

Now that you have identified one simple change you would like to make, can you choose to take one new action today that will move you in the direction you've identified? With that single step, you are on your way.

Bookends

According to Darren Hardy, editor-in-chief of *Success* magazine and author of *The Compound Effect*, when we consciously build our morning and evening routines to support our path to success, we create "bookends" for a successful life.[37] The moments after you open your eyes each morning represent an opportunity to reflect and prepare, and the moments when you shift from work to rest each night represent an opportunity to reflect and regroup. I have come to see these two bookends as critical supports to a leader's effort to achieve growth and change.

> *"Nobody can go back and start a new beginning, but anyone can start today and make a new ending." – Maria Robinson, Ireland's first female president*

Paying attention to the two bookends to your day, the start and the finish, is perhaps the simplest and most effective first step to putting self-awareness to work. The goal of bookending your day is to train yourself to be more focused during your productive time, and to fully immerse yourself in recharging during your relaxation/family time.

> *Increasing our mindfulness during the two bookends of each day can greatly increase our ability to effectively respond to events throughout the day.*

British psychologist Alan Baddeley has proposed that our working memory contains an episodic buffer. That buffer is a system for temporary storage of information from other parts of the working memory, and its responsible for integrating that information and maintaining a sense of time, so we can remember events in a chronological sequence. Baddeley theorizes that conscious awareness is the principal mode we use to retrieve information from the episodic buffer.[38] That means the more we pay attention to what we are experiencing, the better equipped we are to search the buffer for effective choices.

Extrapolating from Baddeley's line of thinking, if we begin each day by being more conscious of the day, we increase our power to influence the outcomes of the day. Our consciousness is a tool that allows us to pull together information from our working memory that we can reflect on and use in planning the future. When we consciously give our attention to one experience, feeling, thought, or memory over another, we are in effect telling our working memory's episodic buffer which information to prioritize for our use throughout the day.

Bookending your day gives you double-loop feedback, an open-ended cycle in which you plan actions, examine those actions, and reflect on those actions. Your reflections at the end of one day then inform your plans at the start of the next day, as you begin the cycle again.

How then, can you make the best use of your day's bookends?

Morning Bookend: I suggest starting each day with the intention to recognize that you are alive another day, that you will take full advantage of this by focusing on moving toward your values, that you will leverage your self-awareness to increase your effectiveness, and that you will commit to being the person you wish to be. With that in mind, I then recommend reflecting on the first step you will take each day to bring you closer to the most important change goal you have identified.

Evening Bookend: I suggest a daily self-debrief at the end of each workday. Don't wait until bedtime. Signal to yourself a boundary between your productive time and your recharging time. It can be a challenge to commit to this. When you get home, you may be tired, your mind may be racing, or your family may be eager to interact with you. Yet that's exactly what the debrief will help you with. Taking a deliberate moment to be alone with yourself and reflect on your day can be restful, help you put your thoughts into perspective, and prepare you to be more present with your loved ones.

Self-reflection allows you to gauge your progress toward change. When you're reflecting it helps to consider three areas: 1) responding, 2) expanding, and 3) envisioning. That is, 1) review how you *responded* to the day's opportunities, 2) *expand* on the thoughts and feelings you experienced during those responses, and 3) *envision* how you can use today's responses as learning experiences to grow tomorrow. Don't judge your responses, just notice where you are on the path between your old choices and your new ones.

At the end of your evening debrief, contemplate how you want to replicate, improve, or increase your new choices tomorrow. Then all of that information will be at your disposal in the morning as you begin a new day with reflection.

Open Yourself to Magic Moments Each Day

Sometimes the first step to take so you can move in the direction of change is to keep your eyes open for opportunities. Remember Amy from Chapter Four? She was the university administrator with a new career goal in public relations who began noticing uncanny coincidences that seemed to carry her toward her goal. I don't believe that was mere chance, but was instead *synchronicity*.

The first assignment I had given Amy was to envision herself in her new role, a process called *initiation*. Then I asked Amy to create an *intention* by picturing a story of what her future in that role would look like. With that intention in mind, she was more prepared to uncover opportunities she would not have noticed before, opportunities synchronous with her intention. She wanted to work in PR, so when someone called with a fundraising idea she reacted to it the way a PR person would, by taking a single step in the direction of turning that idea into a public relations opportunity. All she did was suggest the opportunity to a superior, and she was off, moving in a new direction!

Amy continues to gain greater understanding of her intentions, so that she can continue to invite magical moments of synchronicity in which the universe seems to line up for her.

When you envision your future and pay attention to experiences that align with your vision—whether you call it synchronicity or the power of intention—and make choices based on that attention, you are bound to move toward your vision. If you wish to change, I suggest you take advantage of at least one synchronistic moment each day.

"Some scientists see a theoretical grounding for synchronicity in quantum physics, fractal geometry, and chaos theory. They are finding that the isolation and separation of objects from each other is more apparent than real; at deeper levels, everything—atoms, cells, molecules, plants, animals, people— participates in a sensitive, flowing web of information." - Meg Lundstrom, "A Wink From the Cosmos"

To take advantage of synchronicity, all you have to do is pay attention each day and say "yes" to one opportunity you might have missed before. Saying "yes" can mean doing something as simple as listening to an idea that resonates with you and then taking a step in the direction of that idea. You might tell the person who shared it, "I like that idea. Tell me more." Or you might spend five minutes online, researching subjects related to the new idea. Or you might ask someone to draft a one-page proposal on the new idea. Saying "yes" to an unexpected opportunity is another way to take just one small step in the new direction you want to go.

"It's a poor sort of memory that only works backwards." - Lewis Carroll, *Through the Looking Glass*

Stay Awake

Even small steps to change ask us to pay more conscious attention to our days, to take ourselves off autopilot and actively engage in the one new behavior we've chosen. This requires us to flip the "on" switch of the observing self. I find it helpful to call on my awareness the moment I wake in the morning: to become aware of my breathing, to spend a moment in gratitude, to remind myself what is truly important to me as I prepare to step into my day.

Take advantage of small opportunities to wake up your observing self. When you shower, focus on how warm your shower feels, how great the soap smells, how refreshing it is to feel clean. Pay attention to your thoughts. The average shower takes about eight minutes. That's a meaningful chunk of time to open yourself to what the day's experiences have to offer.

I advise leaders not to jump into multitasking first thing in the morning, which squanders the opportunity to start the day in mindfulness. Instead, try enjoying that first cup of coffee or bite of breakfast without the distraction of the TV, newspaper, Internet, email, or voicemail. Savor the smell of your coffee as it brews, its taste on your tongue, the warmth of the cup in your hands, the sensation percolating through your body. Add that five minutes to your eight-minute shower and you have thirteen minutes of mindfulness. Now you'll be in a more receptive frame of mind to attend to email, your calendar, meetings, and whatever else the day has in store.

On average, most professionals attend 61.8 meetings a month. If your days are packed, all the more reason to find every opportunity to bring your body back into the moment. If you don't, it becomes all too easy to respond on autopilot. If you don't take every opportunity to be mindful of your internal and external experience, you risk failing to notice opportunities. Those opportunities are the ones that invite you to try out your new behavior.

Every encounter presents an opportunity to move toward your values. Here are three questions to ask yourself when you see an opportunity:

1. What is the single most important change I'm trying to make right now?
2. Is this an opportunity to engage in a new style, technique, or behavior?
3. What will it look like at this moment to successfully take one step toward that change?

If you need a boost to get into a mindful mindset, try one of the Mindful Moments from this book. Here's another, adapted with permission from Alfred James' *Pocket Mindfulness* blog:[31]

MINDFUL MOMENT #7
LISTENING

Objective: This exercise is designed to open your ears to sound in a nonjudgmental way. So much of what we hear on a daily basis is influenced by memories of past experiences. Mindful listening helps us leave the past behind and come into a neutral, present awareness.

1. Select an unfamiliar piece of music from your collection, or from the Internet or radio.
2. Use headphones if you can.
3. Close your eyes.
4. Play the music without thinking about the genre or artist. For the duration of the song focus only on all the intricacies of the sounds, nothing else. Allow yourself to become fully entwined with what is playing, without preconceptions or judgments.
5. If judgments come up unbidden, that's okay. Don't judge the judgment. Just notice that you have left the music, and then come back to it.

By becoming mindful of who we are, where we are, and what we're doing, we cultivate a truer awareness of our being. When we fully inhabit our body and pay attention to its five senses, we improve our ability to identify and reduce stress and anxiety, and we open ourselves to reconnecting with our values and purpose.

Stay Energized

Staying awake to the opportunities each day offers is challenging. We don't have unlimited energy. When we juggle too much—including too many thoughts—the cumulative effect is loss of energy and loss of capacity to respond. If you want to stay engaged in your day, do your best to connect with four sources of energy:

MAINTAIN YOUR FOUR ENERGY QUADRANTS

1. Physically energized
2. Emotionally connected
3. Mentally focused
4. Aligned with your values

We are more likely to maintain the above four energy quadrants when we focus on the now. When we dwell on what happened five minutes or five days ago, or worry about what will happen later today or tomorrow, we become less present in the now. That's when we run the risk of becoming automatic human doings instead of conscious human beings, selling ourselves short and becoming less useful to the organizations we lead.

Scott was the chief strategy officer for a global manufacturing firm, and he was a brilliant problem solver. If nobody could find a solution to a big challenge, they called Scott. He had an IQ that put him in the top two percent, and he had a gift for seeing paths where others only saw obstacles. Unfortunately, he did not suffer fools gladly, and according to him "most people are fools." The day he took the CEO to task in a meeting, insisting the CEO was wrong, was the day that almost did him in.

As Scott worked on self-awareness, he realized that he dealt with anxiety by displaying intellectual arrogance as a way to distance himself from others. That explained why he could not let go of his argument with the CEO. Such behavior was effective at giving him the psychic distance he craved, but it was ineffective at helping him maintain the relationships he needed if he wanted people to keep calling on him to solve problems.

Scott worked on his awareness and noticed that his desire for distance was more likely to result in derailing behaviors when he was frustrated, tired, or fearful that he could not solve the problem presented to him. When facing such dilemmas, his default setting was to work harder, ruminating on the problem without breaks, which led to exhaustion, which made him even more likely to react to others with distance, condescension, and arrogance.

Scott chose to make one change. Whenever he noticed himself ruminating, he stopped taking that as a cue to work harder. Instead, he switched gears and engaged in an activity that would give him positive energy. He created a list of energizing choices for all four quadrants:

1) if he was losing physical energy he might eat or exercise, 2) if he was losing mental energy he might read an article, 3) if he was losing emotional energy he might visit with his wife, 4) if he felt drained by a lack of alignment with his values he might pause to reconnect with them.

Scott set a goal to reduce his hindering reactions by thirty percent. It might not sound like much on the face of it, but a shift like that can have a profound impact. Imagine you reduced your resistance to making time to work out, with a goal to exercise thirty percent more than you do now. Would that have a significant impact on your life? Of course it would.

Is there one new choice in your life that, if you were to make it thirty percent of the time, would increase your energy and make it less likely for you to engage in derailing behavior?

INCREASE YOUR ENERGY WITH ONE NEW CHOICE A DAY

1. Take out a pad and pen.
2. Create four columns with four headings:
   - Physical
   - Mental
   - Emotional
   - Values
3. Under each heading, write down a new choice you can easily make that will positively increase your energy in that quadrant.
4. Whenever your observing self notices that you are losing energy in one of the four quadrants, pick just one of your ideas and act on it.

Your Journey Begins

Since aware leadership is a journey, not a destination, there's no point in running headlong toward the finish line. If you want to succeed at applied self-awareness, take small steps, make incremental changes, and embrace one new choice at a time. That is how you will create the time and energy you need to be awake to every moment, every challenge, every opportunity. Taking this journey slow and steady will help you navigate the best path to your most aware self.

Approach this journey the way you journey through music you love. When you listen to a favorite song, you're in no rush to reach the end. Savor the music of self-awareness in all its variety: harmonies, high notes, low notes, repeating refrains, even those sections where you can hear the musician's fingers sliding over the guitar strings or the intake of breath as the singer struggles to reach a note. Such is the complex symphony of self-awareness.

A WORD TO THE AWARE LEADER:

I love those who can smile in trouble, who can gather strength from distress, and grow brave by reflection. 'Tis the business of little minds to shrink, but they whose heart is firm, and whose conscience approves their conduct, will pursue their principles unto death.

—Leonardo da Vinci

THIRTEEN

YOUR FIRST STEP:

W.I.S.D.O.M. — WHAT I SHALL DO ON MONDAY

In this book's introduction, I proposed a challenge: to be prepared by the end of the book to name one step you plan to take to put your self-awareness into action. That time has come. We're at the end of the book. I suggest you select one thing that resonates with you, which you feel you are likely to actually do. Is there a new step that pops into your head as a no-brainer, one you can remember without going back through this book or through your notes to look it up? That's probably a good choice—though I recommend you then look it up anyway, just to clarify your plan and make it real.

I don't want you to walk away without something concrete written down, so below is a list of suggestions for possible first steps, along with where you can find them in the book. If you're new to the practice of self-awareness, I suggest picking your new step from *Box #1: Choices to Build Self-Awareness*. Pick something you can easily incorporate into your life by making one simple daily adjustment. You don't need to focus on the new step all day long, though I do recommend taking action on your new step at least once a day.

#1 — CHOICES TO BUILD SELF-AWARENESS

- Create your personal vision by doing the "After the Miracle Happens" exercise. – Chapter Two
- Familiarize yourself with your default settings. – Chapter Three
- Identify personal scripts you have formed to deal with your significant life experiences. – Chapter Three
- Recall the key influences and influencers in your life. – Chapter Three
- Learn your derailing behaviors. – Chapter Five
- Complete a list of your values with definitions of what those values mean to you. – Chapter Eight
- Select a Mindful Moment exercise and practice it every day for a week. – Chapters Two, Four, Six, Seven, Eight, Ten, Twelve

When your first step becomes routine for you, move on to another one. Once you become accustomed to the practice of self-awareness, move on to *Box #2* below, *Choices to Maintain Your Self-Awareness*, and select another new step from there. Again, you don't need to act on your new step all day long, but make a move in that direction at least once a day. When that step becomes routine for you, move on to another.

#2 — CHOICES TO MAINTAIN SELF-AWARENESS

- What characteristics about yourself do you negatively judge that you are ready to embrace instead? – Chapter Two
- Which attributes facilitate your success and in what situations? Which attributes hinder your success and in what situations? – Chapter Two
- Become a daily observer of yourself. – Chapter Two
- Build pauses into your day. – Chapter Four

- Practice dealing with problematic thoughts or emotions. – Chapter Seven
- Learn more about yourself by soliciting feedback or completing assessments. – Chapter Eleven
- Bookend each day. – Chapter Twelve
- Select a new Mindful Moment exercise and practice it every day for one week. – Chapters Two, Four, Six, Seven, Eight, Ten, Twelve
-

Just in case the Mindful Moments you have read so far aren't doing it for you today, or you don't want to flip pages but do want a first step to take away with you, try this one:

MINDFUL MOMENT #8
FULLY EXPERIENCE YOUR ROUTINE

Objective: The intention of this exercise is to cultivate contentedness in the moment, rather than getting caught up in the feeling of wanting something to end so you can get on to doing the next thing. It might even make you enjoy some of those boring daily chores too.

1. Choose a routine activity that you typically do almost unconsciously, without really noticing your actions. For example, cleaning your house.
2. For one week, or the next time you do that activity, make a point to pay attention to every detail of what you're doing. So, if it's housecleaning, feel and become the motion of sweeping the floor, notice the muscles you use when scrubbing the dishes, observe the formation of dirt on the windows and see if you can create a more efficient way of removing it.
3. Make sure you don't spend your whole time merely pushing toward or thinking about the finish line, or how relieved you will be when you're done, or what the next activity of the day is. Instead, stay aware of every step of the

activity and enjoy your progress. Take the activity beyond a routine by merging with it physically and mentally.

Self-Awareness Is the Pursuit of Happiness

This book is about the journey of self-awareness, but if you draw an arrow from that journey to its goal, the arrow will point to happiness. Think back on all you've read, and I believe the truth will come through as loud and clear for you as it does for me: self-awareness is the key to self-acceptance, which is the key to love. The underlying act that determines our satisfaction in life is the expression of love, for ourselves, for others, and for what we do.

We all have experienced love at some point— of ourselves, of others, of what we do. Let the memory of that experience move you in the direction of self-awareness. That will enable you to rediscover love again and again.

What often gets in the way of expressing love, and therefore gets in the way of contentment, is fear. The only way to get past fear-based emotions is to observe them, accept them, and move through them. We do this by engaging the observing self to pay attention to our internal and external life without judgment.

Becoming a nonjudgmental observer of the self requires willpower. If we want to become self-aware, we must accept that we won't always be comfortable. This is not easy because humans are programmed to avoid pain, but it can be done if we commit and keep taking steps in the direction of change. This is how we become aware leaders, by doing what is hard.

It takes practice to develop the skills to notice what is truly going on within us and around us, instead of automatically reacting to our judgments about what's happening. Practicing this sort of awareness involves *intentionality*. Intentionality means focusing the right skills in the right direction, which will take us in incremental steps from automatic behavior to conscious action. We increase our orientation toward success when we relish awareness of our experience at all times, because that is when we have the clearest view of all the choices available to us.

Good guidance is invaluable as we embark on the journey of the aware leader. Mentors, coaches, teachers, and spiritual leaders are a few who can assist us in uncovering our personal narratives and developing good practices. If you typically resist asking for help, you need to break that barrier. Contrary to common belief, helpless people don't ask for help, leaders do.

You don't have to wait for some life-shattering experience to reach the epiphany of self-awareness. This can be a positive daily experience. Self-awareness asks you to commit to accepting yourself and your life daily as a means to joy and success.

It is in your power to transform yourself into the leader you described in your personal vision. It only requires that you take one step in that direction every day. So long as you keep moving in the direction you've chosen, you cannot help but arrive.

What are you doing in your daily life that is moving you toward becoming the person you envision? What are you doing in your daily life that is moving you away from that vision? What is the first step you will take on Monday to bring you closer to becoming the great leader you know you can be?

A WORD TO THE AWARE LEADER:

"Your visions will become clear only when you can look into your own heart. Who looks outside, dreams; who looks inside, awakes."

— Carl Jung

GRATITUDE AND ACKNOWLEDGMENTS

The poet Audre Lorde reminds us, "There are no new ideas. There are only new ways of making them felt." In that spirit, I humbly offer my gratitude to the people who have influenced and shaped my life and to those thought-leaders who have chosen to help all of us on our journeys to self-awareness.

My intention behind writing *The Aware Leader* is to introduce readers to what they need to know about themselves if they yearn for true success, and to share some of the many possibilities for pursuing that self-knowledge.

What led me to pursue this purpose?

My first and foremost motivation for reaching out to others with this message has been my own personal journey. I was four years old, riding in our family's 1957 Ford Fairlane on Hemphill Avenue on a blazing hot day in Fort Worth, Texas, when I scared the bejeebers (my mom's word) out of my parents. Every time we stopped at an intersection, I leaned out of the car window to talk to people in the other waiting cars. Since then, my interest in people has never waned.

When I reflect on the most influential memories of my life, it is images not of events but of people that emerge: parents, brother, children, spouses, friends, foes, teachers, mentors, bosses, colleagues, clients, and even momentary acquaintances who have crossed my path. Everyone I have encountered along the way has added to the joy, sorrow, challenge, peace, energy, weariness, love, loss, and triumph I have been privileged to experience in life. In experiencing all of these emotions there is no regret. There is only gratitude.

This book evolved not only from the enriching experience of discovering myself through observation, but also from allowing others to give me the gift of their observations about me and from witnessing other people on their own journeys to self-knowledge. Many thanks to all who have contributed to my growth by giving their understanding to me and allowing me to learn about them.

It has been a true gift to have the support of my family, people who have always believed in me even when that was hard. My deepest thanks to my sons, Reiss and Geoff, who continue to encourage and challenge me, and to my mother, who always knew I had a story to tell.

Twenty years ago it was my honor to work with Dr. Irwin Gadol as my therapist. He passed in 2007, much too soon, but his impact on my life and the lives of many others continues. His insight and compassion were rare gifts. My journey to self-awareness had its truest beginning when I met him. I'm committed to passing on what I can of his legacy.

My friend of thirty-plus years, Micki Grimland, pushed, prodded, and challenged me to write this book. Thanks to her for providing invaluable counsel, suggestions, and encouragement.

I offer a big shout-out to Georgetown University's Leadership Coaching; its founder and my coach, Chris Wahl; the Class of Sweet 16; and to all those who shared their wisdom with me during that incredible learning opportunity. To every person I have had the opportunity to coach, I express my humble gratitude for giving me as much as or more insight than I have shared with you. The sacred space of coaching is not lost on me. My respect for all of you is without bounds. As I'm fond of telling anyone who will listen, the best hour I spend every day is the one when I get to coach an executive.

From my parents, I received the DNA for intellectual and interpersonal curiosity. The DNA for writing, however, was either not honed or not strongly present in any chromosome. Cara Lopez Lee and Mark Graham lifted this book up. Cara translated my words and ideas into readable material, always capturing who I am. Mark provided sage advice every step of the way. My thanks to both of them for believing in this project.

Many thanks to everyone who supported the idea of this book and provided feedback on both the ideas and presentation.

Each and every person I have met along my journey has taught me something. Thank you all, and let us continue to walk in the dream and pursuit of greater awareness of all our many wondrous selves.

RICHARD METHENY, 2019

RESOURCES

1, David Zes and Dana Landis. *A Better Return on Self-Awareness*. The Korn Ferry Institute, August 2013

2. https://fortune.com/2018/04/19/best-ceos-fortune-greatest-leaders/

3. Nate Boaz and Erica Ariel Fox. Change Leader, Change Thyself. *McKinsey Quarterly*, March 2014

4. J.P. Flaum, Managing Partner, Green Peak Partners, https://greenpeakpartners.com/wp-content/uploads/2018/09/Green-Peak_Cornell-University-Study_What-predicts-success.pdf. , 2010

5. Daniel T. Holt, Achilles A. Armenakis, Hubert S. Feild and Stanley G. Harris. Readiness for Organizational Change: The Systematic Development of a Scale. *Journal of Applied Behavioral Science*, 2007; 43; 232

6. Jon L. Pierce and Donald G. Gardner. Self-Esteem Within the Work and Organizational Context: A Review of the Organization-Based Self-Esteem Literature. *Journal of Management*, 2004 30: 591

7. Takashi Nakao, Mayo Mitsumoto, Hitomi Nashiwa, Masahiro Takamura, Satoko Tokunaga, Makoto Miyatani, Hideki Ohira, Kaori Katayama, Akane Okamoto and Yu Watanabe. *Self-Knowledge Reduces Conflict by Biasing One of Plural Possible Answers. Personality and Social Psychology Bulletin*, 2010 36: 455

8. Francesc Borrell-Carrió, MD and Ronald M. Epstein, MD. Preventing Errors in Clinical Practice: A Call for Self-Awareness. *Annals of Family Medicine*, Vol. 2, No. 4, July/August 2004

9. Emily Pronin, Daniel Y. Lin, Lee Ross. Stanford University. The Bias Blind Spot: Perceptions of Bias in Self Versus Others. *Personality and Social Psychology Bulletin*, March 2002 28

10. *Being Wrong: Adventures in the Margin of Error.* Kathryn Shulz. Ecco, June 8, 2010

11. Wood, W., Tam, L., & Witt, M.G. (2005). Changing Circumstances, Disrupting Habits. *Journal of Personality and Social Psychology*, 88(6), 918-933

12. *The Stories We Live By: Personal Myths and the Making of the Self.* Dan P. MacAdams. William Morrow & Co, January 3, 1997

13. Bryan Walsh. The Upside of Being an Introvert (and Why Extroverts are Overrated). *Time*, February 6, 2012

14. *Coaching: Evoking Excellence in Others.* James Flaherty. Oxford, UK: Butterworth-Heinemann, 1999, p.163

15. *The Hogan Guide: Interpretation and Use of Hogan Inventories.* Robert Hogan, Joyce Hogan, Rodney Warrenfelz. Hogan Assessment Systems, 2007, p.199

16. David Foster Wallace on Life and Work. Adapted from a commencement speech given by David Foster Wallace to the 2005 graduating class at Kenyon College. *Wall Street Journal*, September 19, 2008

17. Dan Hurley. Grandma's Experiences Leave a Mark on Your Genes. *Discover*. May, 2013

18. Dan P. McAdams, Department of Psychology and School of Education and Social Policy, Northwestern University, and Kate C. McLean, Department of Psychology, Western Washington University. *Current Directions in Psychological Science*, a Journal of the Association for Psychological Science, 22(3) 233–238, 2013

19. *The Monk Who Sold His Ferrari.* Robin Sharma. HarperSanFrancisco, April 21, 1999

20. V. W. Donaldson. A clinical study of visualization on depressed white blood cell count in medical patients. *Applied Psychophysiology and Biofeedback.* June, 2000; 25(2):117-28

21. Jose Martin-Albo, Juan L. Nuñez, Evelia Dominguez, Jaime Leon, Jose M. Tomas. *Relationships between intrinsic motivation, physical self-concept and satisfaction with life: A longitudinal study.* Department of Psychology and Sociology, University of Zaragoza, Zaragoza Spain; Department of Psychology and Sociology, University of Las Palmas de Gran Canaria, Las Palmas, Spain; Department of Behavioral Sciences Methodology, University of Valencia, Valencia, Spain. Accepted December 12, 2011

22. Noah Shachtman. In Silicon Valley, Meditation Is No Fad. It Could Make Your Career. *Wired.* June 18, 2013

23. Tony Schwartz, Catherine McCarthy. Manage Your Energy, Not Your Time. *Harvard Business Review*. October, 2007

24. Robert Hogan, Ph.D.; Joyce Hogan, Ph.D. *Hogan Development Survey Manual*. Hogan Assessment Systems, 1997

25. *The Extraordinary Leader: Turning Good Managers into Great Leaders*. John Zenger and Joseph Folkman. McGraw-Hill Education 2nd edition, May, 2009

26. Peter Salovey, Yale University; John D. Mayer, University of New Hampshire. *Emotional Intelligence*. Baywood Publishing Company, Inc, 1990

27. *The Emotional Brain: The Mysterious Underpinnings of Emotional Life*. Joseph LeDoux. Simon & Schuster, March 27, 1998

28. *Descartes' Error: Emotion, Reason, and The Human Brain*. Antonio R. Damasio. Penguin Books, September 27, 2005

29. *The Progress Principle: Using Small Wins to Ignite Joy, Engagement, and Creativity at Work*. Teresa Amabile and Steven Kramer. Harvard Business Review Press, July 19, 2011

30. *ACT Made Simple: An Easy-To-Read Primer on Acceptance and Commitment Therapy*. Russ Harris. New Harbinger Publications, November 1, 2009. P.9

31. Alfred James. 6 Mindfulness Exercises You Can Try Today. *Pocket Mindfulness blog*. http://www.pocketmindfulness.com/6-mindfulness-exercises-you-can-try-today/. 2015

32. *Choice Theory: A New Psychology of Personal Freedom*. William Glasser, M.D. HarperCollins Publishers, January 6, 1999

33. *Apples Are Square: Thinking Differently About Leadership*. Susan and Thomas Kuczmarski. Book Ends Publishing, 2012

34. Norbert Schwarz, University of Michigan, and Gerd Bohner, University of Mannheim, Feelings and their Motivational Implications: Moods and the Action Sequence, in P. Gollwitzer, & J. A. Bargh (Editors). *The psychology of action: Linking cognition and motivation to behavior* (pp. 119-145). New York: Guilford 1996.

35. *The Five-Factor Model of Personality: Theoretical Perspectives*. Jerry S. Wiggins, Ph.D (Editor). The Guilford Press, March 15, 1996

36. *Facilitating Organization Change: Lessons from Complexity Science*. Edwin E. Olson, Glenda H. Eoyang. Pfeiffer, February 7, 2001

37. *The Compound Effect*. Darren Hardy. Vanguard Press. October 2, 2012

38. Alan Baddeley. The episodic buffer: a new component in working memory? *Trends In Cognitive Sciences* — Vol. 4, No. 11, November 2000

Made in the USA
Columbia, SC
06 January 2020

86421602R00114